G000256993

# THE AUTHORITY GUIDE TO
# DEVELOPING HIGH
# PERFORMANCE TEAMS

How to develop brilliant teams and reap the rich
rewards of effective collaboration in the workplace

## ANDREW JENKINS

**The Authority Guide to Developing High-performance Teams**

How to develop brilliant teams and reap the rich rewards of effective collaboration in the workplace

© Andrew Jenkins

ISBN 978-1-909116-92-4

eISBN 978-1-909116-93-1

Published in 2017 by Authority Guides

authorityguides.co.uk

The right of Andrew Jenkins to be identified as the author of this work has been asserted by him in accordance with the Copyright, Designs and Patents Act 1988.

A CIP record of this book is available from the British Library.

All rights reserved. No part of this book may be reproduced, stored in a retrieval system, or transmitted in any form or by any means, electronic, mechanical, photocopying, recording or otherwise, without the prior written permission of the publisher.

No responsibility for loss occasioned to any person acting or refraining from action as a result of any material in this publication can be accepted by the author or publisher.

Printed in the United Kingdom.

# Contents

Trust is the glue that binds people together
and the lubricant which allows energy and
passion to flow.

Stephen M R Covey

# Introduction

## A case for team building

To build a great business today isn't just about having a great product or service and an efficient means of producing it. In today's world, that's not a differentiator, it's a given.

Also while KPIs and business metrics are important for business effectiveness, they aren't the be-all-and-end-all for success. To make a real difference means working together to build a great high-performing team.

### Changing from the inside out

I believe any team with the right people, input and direction can learn to become a high-performing team. But it doesn't involve some extrinsic magic formula that you apply from the 'outside in'. You can't become a high-performing team that way. It's more subtle than that. I believe that becoming an effective team is an intrinsic and organic process that takes time (and teamwork) to nurture.

It's about changing people from the inside out. You must work on yourselves. That requires a willingness to grow as individuals and as a team. It also needs you to commit to a process designed around your needs. That's what this book does.

## Why this book?

This *Authority Guide to Developing High-performance Teams* gets that ball rolling. It helps any leadership or management team dynamically to learn to build collaborative skills together. By learning and developing these skills and qualities, teams can grow into becoming high performing and resilient. Business success then follows.

The guide is designed to be used as a toolkit for leaders, managers, consultants, trainers and facilitators to get the most out of working with newly formed teams or well-established teams, leadership teams, management teams or *any* sort of team for that matter.

It is *not* a book about improving *what* you do as a business person. It is *not* about business acumen or skills, or about business practice, how to get more customers, leadership governance or process.

These aspects of business are essential, of course, and this book assumes that those qualities are being (or have been) acquired through experience. However, even if managers are highly competent, that doesn't mean they'll make an effective manager of people. That requires completely different skills.

So, this book helps leaders and managers of teams to develop effective teamwork skills. It will also help people to grow into *who* they are meant to be as individuals and to make a difference at work.

## Building a great team

Becoming a great high-performance team needs to become a goal to which are you are dedicated. Planning to take time out is essential. Moreover, to get there you will need to:

- commit to developing together as a team
- be humble and vulnerable with one another – letting go of ego
- learn how to collaborate, cohere and boost your emotional intelligence
- work towards identifying and reaching your 'big goals'.

Ultimately, having developed into a high-performance team means that you can then get on and focus on running your business successfully without having to spend unproductive time working through people issues.

Good leadership is about creating enterprises that flourish. However, it is certainly possible to create workplaces in which everybody connected with that enterprise thrives and in which everybody matters. There is a lot of evidence to suggest that it is these organisations that flourish the most.

All this starts with great teamwork. So, that's why you need this book.

## Using this *Authority Guide* with its supporting website

This book is unique in that it works hand in hand with my supporting website (pdx-consulting.com/resources.htm).

The benefit to you as the reader is that all the worksheets referred to in this book are downloadable in ready-to-use format, directly from the website listed on the previous page.

I suggest that to get the full sense of using any of the exercises in this book that you are interested in, then download the supporting worksheets from the website and read in conjunction with this book.

Each chapter in this book is designed to have a practical stand-alone team-building theme. Specific easy-to-follow activities, exercises, models and tools develop distinct teamwork skills, qualities and attributes.

The book's chapters are arranged logically. Starting with building trust, each chapter follows in order and progressively builds on the previous topic. The sum of all the chapters will lead to the creation of a successful high-performing team.

In the final chapter, I provide some typical team development programmes and event suggestions with approximate timings, along with other useful resources.

I have successfully used and honed all the content in this book over many years with teams of all shapes, sizes and seniority. So, it's all been tried and tested.

By using this approach, I believe that you will help teams to do their very best work.

# Build trust

## Why is trust so important?

No team leadership quality is more important than trust. But purposefully building trust in teams is rarely undertaken.

I believe that good leadership is about creating enterprises that flourish. It is certainly possible to create workplaces in which everybody connected with that enterprise thrives. To do this, leadership teams need to care about both a higher purpose and their people. These types of leaders build cultures and teams based on trust and the genuine caring of others. They are not driven by bottom-line profit for its own sake, but create value by making a difference and by making the world better.

Trust is applicable to all teams. If you trust people in your team and show that you believe in them, everyone benefits. Trust can transform individual lives and teams and make the future success of a business much more likely.

So, trust is the foundation upon which high-performance cultures and effective teams are built, whereas distrust ultimately leads to dysfunction and low performance.

## Team trust review

On my website you will find the 'Team trust review assessment' worksheet 1.1, which is a tool designed to gauge the level of current team trust. Applicable to any team of any size in any business, it asks team members to rate issues such as whether they ask for help or refuse it.

As the facilitator, download and email the tool to team members in advance. When I run workshops, I ask team members to spend ten minutes or so completing this on their own as pre-work. I tell them not to share this with their colleagues. Each person then brings their completed assessment review to the team day, where the results can be collated and shared when appropriate.

Because individual members are completing this, it's subjective but once everybody's answers are collated, it provides the team with some objective data that will help them to analyse their level of trust with one another.

## Telling stories about trust

Fundamentally, trust is about learning to be comfortable by opening yourself up a bit. Trust goes beyond basic needs such as self-preservation, survival, protection, defensiveness, political game playing and self-centred ego. So, building trust as a team requires learning higher-growth-based values. By doing this, teams that trust each other develop the courage to be personally open enough to admit the truth about themselves – flaws, weaknesses, failures and fears. In short, they learn to do without pretence or masks.

Learning to trust means taking a risk by removing our masks and being honest to ourselves and to others. It's having the courage to genuinely say any of the following:

- You're right – your viewpoint is better.

- I was wrong – I made a mistake. What can I do differently?

- I'm not sure. Can I have your advice on this?

- It's my fault.

- I'm sorry.

- I trust your judgement.

- Would you mind giving me a hand?

- What can I do to help?

- I couldn't have done it without you.

- I'm all ears.

Below is an exercise based on 'appreciative inquiry', first developed by David Cooperrider and Suresh Sirvastva at Western Reserve University in the late 1980s. Its story-telling approach is based on focusing attention on what works – the positive core – and on what people really care about.

It is especially useful to promote strong connections and relationships between people working in teams. The objective is to draw out personal strengths and motivations that then become profound assets for team learning.

## 'Appreciative inquiry', stories that build trust – exercise

Here's a simple yet engaging and profound first step that starts to develop team trust by telling stories. Use this as part of an initial offsite team-building day. It helps people begin to safely reveal aspects of their lives that others probably won't know. Individuals learn to let down their guard and give people a glimpse into what has shaped them into who they are today.

### Here's how it works...

In a relaxed setting with everyone seated in a circle (or on comfy settees), have each person take it in turns talking briefly about:

- a job or experience that formed you
- your biggest mistake and positive learning outcome
- a profound experience
- a person in your life who has influenced you and why.

Alternatively, you can ask them to tell stories about the family they grew up in and what was fundamental, important, difficult or challenging as they grew up – and what it taught them.

Nothing too deep, secret or traumatic need be shared. Remember to tell your team members that the intention of the exercise is for each person to reveal something positive and personal and relevant to the group. Emphasise clearly that it certainly isn't a touchy-feely exercise or a group hug-in!

People are always amazed at what comes up and the level of honesty expressed. Remember, too, that a minority of people will report having had no issues while growing up or, alternatively, will share quite personal things – both of which are, of course, fine.

As the group learns new aspects about each other, the exercise also helps the team to cohere and quickly creates new-found respect and understanding for each another. It also breaks down negative assumptions unwittingly held about other team members.

It is vital that the group listens respectfully and appreciatively to each other. After each story is shared, encourage them to gently ask questions if they wish. If there is just silence, it's important to acknowledge what has been said with a simple smile and a thank you.

Don't rush this exercise. For a team of around 6–8 people, this could easily take two hours or so. For a larger group, it may be a half-day chunk of time including an ice-breaker.

Finally, capture the group's learnings and summarise on a flip chart.

## A few examples

• One team I worked with were collectively amazed at the strong connections to their family roots they had all felt. They found the exercise useful as none of them had ever talked about such things to each other before.

The managing director was struck by the strong influence that his father had had on shaping his destiny. His mother had taught him the value of stability and love.

The finance director talked about being a slow learner at school but, through the support and acceptance of her parents, had matured into an intelligent and successful financier.

The sales director mentioned her family falling on hard times when she and her siblings were young and how that had helped them become a tight-knitted family. That experience helps her today to believe that her team will get through hard times at work when sales are down during a recession.

- A manager in another team mentioned how, since his painful divorce, he had been distrustful of others and that the trust exercise had made him realise this for the first time. He committed himself to change in the future.

- A team leader told how a close call with death following a motorbike accident had made him radically turn around for the better his poor behaviour and bad attitudes towards others. This opened the door for him becoming an inspiring leader of individuals and teams.

## Personality profiling tools

Having done the above exercise, I recommend that you then develop trust further by using a comprehensive personality or behavioural profiling tool. Myers Briggs (MBTI®), TotalSDI, DISC® or Insights are all useful tools and well researched, although my own preference is Myers Briggs. In their own way, each profiling tool provides an objective approach to understanding how each person in the team ticks (see Additional resources on page 78).

Because these are generic profiling tools, they provide a common language for team members to better understand each other. This, in turn, provides a structure for team members to overcome any reluctance to talk about themselves. Strengths and weaknesses can begin to be explored safely around different personality types too. This makes it easier to provide feedback in a non-threating manner within the team. Teams find this a well-worthwhile half-day process.

## Tip

Use a flip chart to capture and visually share all the profiling data. This can then be referred to again during subsequent team-building away days. (If you email me – the address is on my website and at the end of this book – I'll share with you a template you could use to record this information.)

## Components of mutual trust –exercise

The 'trust review' and 'appreciate inquiry' exercise both focused on team members. This next exercise engages the whole team in evaluating their level of mutual trust.

On my website you will find the 'Components of mutual trust' worksheet 1.2. (Reproduced with the kind permission of Richard Barrett from his book *The New Leadership Paradigm*.)

As the facilitator, download and make enough A4 copies for the team to work on in pairs. You have a total of ten smiley faces (strength points) and a total of ten sad faces (weakness points). Allocate these to any of the 12 components of the 'Components of mutual trust' exercise. One or more happy faces can be added to any of the 12 components boxes that you consider are strengths within the team. Do the same with the sad faces, which represent weaknesses or areas for improvement.

Then, work as a team and use a blank A1 (flip chart) the size of the worksheet to capture all pairs' scores.

## Scoring Tip

In any box that contains both happy and smiley faces, then a happy and sad face will cancel each other out. For example, if a box has three happy faces and two sad faces, then you will be left with one happy face in that box.

See a completed 'Components of mutual trust' exercise on my website for reference.

You may find it useful to repeat the team trust review assessment or the above 'Components of mutual trust' exercise a month or two later and compare this to the original assessment. You'll then be able to measure progress of your team and their trust issues.

# Harness conflict

## The importance of dealing with conflict

It can be easy to view conflict within a team as unproductive, emotive and painful. This is because it is often loaded with passion, discord and frustration. So, for these reasons, it is often simply avoided.

However, conflict comprises much more than mere disagreements or personal attacks. High-performing teams view conflict (when dealt with maturely) as healthy, productive and constructive.

If you help teams to engage purposefully in conflict, they will begin to acquire the confidence to resolve issues openly, competently and effectively without upsetting or hurting anyone. Importantly, facing conflict avoids a lack of buy-in, back-room politics and feelings of unresolved issues. If these traits exist, they will lead to low performance and are far more harmful than any heated discussion or open argument.

It's useful for you to highlight to your teams that being able to deal with conflict effectively has many pay-offs. If teams manage disagreements, they can:

- engage in effective meetings and get to the heart of issues quickly

- honour each other's ideas and contributions
- tap into other options and possibilities generated within the team
- be open to healthy mature team behaviours that will eliminate political game playing.

## Relationship development model

The model below was co-created by Janet Gunn and John Sutherland. It is an elegant team tool for you to use when introducing the subject of conflict. This model shows in a simple way the importance of developing healthy interpersonal relationships for us all – at work and in our private lives.

Figure 1 Relationship development model

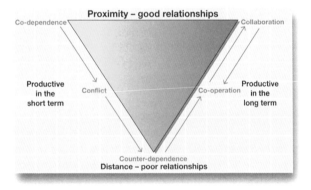

Reproduced with the kind permission of Janet Gunn and John Sutherland. This version is from a training course I attended between 1997 and 1999.

Almost everyone can identify with this model as it depicts lessons learned while growing up in a family. Here's how you can introduce it:

1. As young children, we were all dependent on our parents for our needs.

2. As we went off to school, we began to learn some independence.

3. As teenagers, all of us most likely had to learn how to cope with a degree of conflict.

4. As young adults, we learned to stand on our own two feet.

5. As we developed further, we learned to relate to our parents on a mutual mature footing.

Explain to your team that these five stages follow a basic pattern of codependence, conflict, counter-dependence, co-operation and collaboration. It also readily describes how teams must mature together over time to grow and become high performing.

However, from my experience working with teams, conflict as a subject is often avoided, and counter-intuitively it seems to be more of an issue the higher up in the organisation you go.

Have a close look at Figure 1. The various relationships within teams might be found anywhere on the triangle. They can get stuck at any of these levels and slip back to earlier forms of relationship, too.

Some stay in conflict for their entire duration, with seemingly every contact being difficult and time wasting.

Other relationships may get stuck in a 'Mexican stand-off' type of prolonged independence. Others remain co-dependent.

However, effective teamwork requires an adaptive approach to others based on the needs of the relationship at the time. In the longer term, teams need to work on their relationships to make it around the inverted triangle. High-performing teams spend more time co-operating and collaborating than lower-performing ones.

The bottom of the triangle represents the least degree of relationship we can be in. The top represents the highest degree of relationship, created through either co-dependency or collaboration.

The arrows indicate the healthy flow of development between the five patterns of relating.

The triangle points to the fact that you cannot turn a co-dependent relationship into a co-operative or collaborative one without going through some degree of confrontation or conflict and recognise different viewpoints (independence). There are no short cuts to get to the mutuality side of the triangle.

This is important learning as we can mistakenly view conflict and the growth of independence as negative aspects of relationship development. The truth is that all good relationships experience some degree of confrontation within them, as well as closeness and distance. Harnessed correctly, conflict can be a healthy means of strengthening relationships and combining differences to produce the best outcome for all concerned. This builds confidence that relationships can survive conflict, which in turn builds trust.

The shorter arrow from collaboration back to co-operation indicates that few relationships need to be collaborative long term and may usefully revert to co-operation for most day-to-day tasks.

Finally, the triangle indicates that those relating patterns on the left of the triangle are typically productive in the short term but become ineffective over time. Those relating patterns on the right of the triangle are typically difficult to maintain in the short term, but become increasingly effective over longer periods of time.

## Why relationships get stuck

Talk to your team about common reasons why relationships get stuck at different levels. This will help them to focus back on themselves.

Here are 4 issues around conflict that teams commonly face:

- Not making sufficient time to develop relationships with each other
- Feeling they have little influence over the way members of the team relate to each other
- Having an unresolved conflict with one another
- Not knowing how to challenge others while preserving that relationship

The discussion can then nicely lead you to ask your team: 'What might your issues with conflict be?'

The key to dealing with conflict is to remember that high-performing teams take time to understand each other. They recognise that conflict is healthy and being able to cope with it is a useful and vital skill. Practically speaking, it pays off when teams must make difficult decisions, get through a difficult problem or have to sort out issues together.

## Conflict zones

Having introduced the subject of conflict, you can use this simple model to briefly introduce the notion of healthy and unhealthy conflict.

Figure 2 Conflict zones

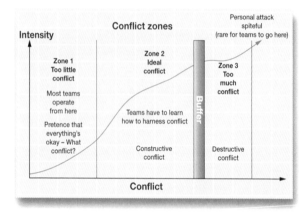

As you can see from the model, too little conflict in teams leads to the pretence that everything is okay (Zone 1). This occurs when issues are not openly debated and too easily brushed off or even swept under the carpet. Interestingly, I have found that most teams are in Zone 1 by default.

Therefore, teams need to learn how to have mature, robust and healthy constructive conversations (Zone 2). This can be uncomfortable but it is necessary.

However, if conflict becomes spiteful and develops into a personal attack, then it has gone too far (Zone 3) and destructive conflict ensues.

Remember to remind the team you are working with that, during heated conflict, team members may cross over to Zone 3 from time to time – into the Buffer Zone (represented by the shaded area). That's acceptable. With awareness, practice and calling this out when it happens, everybody learns how to adjust back into Zone 2 with no harm done. It is also very useful to tell teams that sustained Zone 3 conflict is, in fact, very rare. This will help people to put aside their fears.

## Exploring relationships versus challenges

This simple model has been influenced by one of the core principles of emotional intelligence – relationship management. The weaker the relationship and connection with each other, the harder it is to get important points across. However, the more people learn to expose themselves to challenge and to open up, discuss and debate how each person in the team feels about and handles a challenging conflict situation, the better the solutions and decision making.

Figure 3 Strength of relationships versus level of challenge

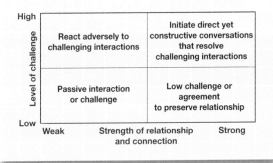

## Exploring relationships versus challenges – exercise

### Purpose

This exercise aims to help the team become more aware of the importance of relationship and challenge for high performance, using the emotional intelligence principle of relationship management.

Furthermore, it develops team awareness of each other's default inclinations to deal with challenge/conflict and to collectively discuss potential areas for improvement.

### Instructions

As the facilitator, download the 'Exploring relationships versus challenges' worksheet 2.1 from my website and then talk the team through the model.

Hand out A4 copies of it and ask each person in the team to mark (with initials) which quadrant would be their default.

As the facilitator working with the team, take each person in turn (starting with the leader) and ask the team which quadrant that person defaults to most of the time.

Ask the person being discussed for their view at the end.

As you deal with each person, come to some sort of consensus as a group about their default quadrant. Plot the results on a flip chart (or an A1 copy of worksheet 2.1).

Together discuss the similarities and differences and how these impact the team at work.

> **Notes**
>
> You can further refine the strength of conflict within each quadrant by placing people either on the outer edges or towards the middle.
>
> Use arrows with short labels or notes to other quadrants to depict movement to other quadrants depending on the context.
>
> *Note – for an alternative approach, refer to Patrick Lencioni's conflict model and exercise in his book* Overcoming the Five Dysfunctions of a Team *(see Further reading).*

## Conflict styles – team discussion

As a next step and to go deeper, I suggest you take a look at the 'Conflict styles team discussion' worksheet 2.2 on my website.

It describes five different approaches, or conflict styles, to how people think and react to the importance of tasks versus relationships. It's derived from a well-known managing conflict model originally created by Thomas-Kilmann. The advantages and disadvantages of each conflict style is briefly outlined in the model.

(For more detail, refer to Kenneth W Thomas's book, *Introduction to Conflict Management*, in which he has usefully developed the conflict model even further. *See* Further reading.)

The level of 'pay-off' – to you and the other party in a conflict situation – is indicated in each of the five areas of the model. The team should pay attention to these.

Here's how they work...

The lowest level of pay-off for both parties is the Avoiding style.

Competing, Compromise and Accommodating styles each provide a medium-level pay-off. The pay-off is either to you, shared, or to the other party.

The highest pay-off to both parties by far comes from the Collaborating style.

Encourage the team to remember these five conflict styles and their labels. It will help them to openly name their own feelings or to call out that that style is being used during a real conflict discussion. This is especially helpful if, or when, team discussions get heated. Practically speaking, in live conflict situations, just remembering the labels of each of the conflict styles and calling out which one is in play at that moment is worthwhile.

Remind the team that high-performing teams usually intentionally aim to use the Collaborating style to problem solve in discussions, to resolve issues and conflicts. Overall, this will lead them to making better decisions. However, other styles may be deliberately selected instead, depending on the circumstances and the goal that needs to be achieved.

So, the Collaborating style is the name of the game, but the trick is being flexible enough to select other styles as and when the situation requires it.

## Conflict styles – team exercise

### Purpose

To help the team objectively identify and understand conflict styles present within the team and when discussing topics, etc.

To encourage team members to be purposeful in how they confront and collaborate with each other, rather than relying on inappropriate default reactive instincts.

To help the team to agree team norms when handling conflict.

## Instructions

As the facilitator, download the 'Conflict styles team discussion' worksheet 2.2 and print out at A1 or recopy onto a flip chart.

With the team, go through each of the five styles and their pay-offs, etc.

Ask the whole team to name (or, rather, give their best educated guess) each other's conflict style within the team – i.e. the style that they think best describes each person's.

Then ask the person being discussed their view on the group's assessment of their style. After making any necessary adjustments, settle on an agreed style.

Write each person's initials in the appropriate area of the template.

## Notes

Team members may express more than one style depending on the context. This is normal. The predominant style can be represented by each person's initials and arrows (with any notes) drawn to represent other styles suggested.

Initials can be placed near the border of two styles too, or on the extreme outer edges to best represent that person and their style.

In addition, if you have used the previous exercise 'Exploring relationships versus challenges' beforehand, you'll notice that they directly map to one another. By doing both exercises, the team's understanding will deepen further.

## Reviewing actions

Place the completed conflict exercises worksheets described above on the floor, together with the 'Relationship development' and 'Conflict zones' models.

Then ask the team to discuss what they have learned. What struck them the most? And how can they adopt the final conflict styles model in practice?

Agree any team rules to do with behaviours and naming conflict styles that help the team to tackle conflict as and when it arises.

Remind the team that this is an important skill and quality if they want to become a high-performing team.

If you have used personality profiling tools with this team at an earlier stage (*see* previous chapter), these can help explain how conflict is handled by different personality profiles. From my experience, Myers Briggs is especially good, as is the 'Strength deployment inventory' (*see* Additional resources on page 78).

Conflict at an individual level can also be picked up in one-to-one coaching sessions.

The next chapter, 'Collaborate', builds on this further.

# Collaborate

## What is collaboration?

This *Authority Guide* has been written so that you can help teams to collaborate effectively. That's what high performance is all about.

However, this chapter allows you to begin to introduce teams to the notion of collaboration. The exercises enable any team to self-learn collaborative skills and apply these for themselves when they are working together.

You'll notice it seamlessly flows on from the 'Harness conflict' chapter. This is deliberate, because knowing how to deal openly with conflict is a necessary part of collaborating.

To get us going, here are some typical collaboration attributes adopted by high-performance teams:

- *Discussions* – Approach topics, problems or issues using dialogue and open discussion, without fear of blame, accusation or personal attack. Instead collectively seek creative decisions that involve the insights, wants and (emotional) needs of team mates.

- *Behaviours* – Actively listen to each other, be curious, acknowledge viewpoints and ask for reactions and views using open language (for example, 'What do you think'? or 'I'm open to other viewpoints'). Build on information and feedback from a variety of sources outside of the team.

- *Attitude* – Be clear, open-minded and respectful. Encourage other insights. Realise that every view is an important resource to help you reach good decisions. Become adept at summarising viewpoints and to monitor understanding and the progress of discussions.

- *Team relationships* – Use team mates to seek effective solutions by drawing on each other's strengths. In so doing, increase team morale and cohesiveness. Believe that you're a great team and that together you will get to the bottom of problems and therefore make good decisions.

- *Conflict* – Work through issues and figure them out. Be confident, motivated and encouraged to find solutions through robust honest conversations. Because the team has built up trust, team members are unafraid to challenge each other.

## Why collaboration is important – Dolphin style

As the facilitator, download a copy of it (worksheet 3.1) from my website and use this simple model to emphasise why team collaboration is so important.

Here's how to do it. Fox-like attributes (*see* top-left box of Figure 4) – that is, being politically aware and clever – are often found in people occupying senior positions in organisations. In the past (when businesses were more hierarchical), Fox-like behaviours were considered stereotypical leadership attributes.

Figure 4 Dolphins, Foxes, Baboons and Sheep

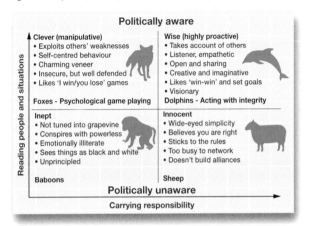

Reproduced with kind permission of Dr Robina Chatham (adapted from Bradley & James), I first saw this model at Cranfield School of Management in 1997–98 during her course on inspirational leadership in the field of corporate politics for IT managers.

Baboon- and Sheep-like behaviours of the politically unaware rarely make it to the senior levels. But such behaviours can be witnessed within teams.

However, today's approach to smart, high-performance teamwork is very much based on developing through collaboration instead. To achieve this means developing your people beyond Baboon-, Sheep- and Fox-like behaviours. These represent default fear-based reactive and instinctive behaviours and habits that have no place in high-performing teams.

Therefore, Dolphin-style attributes (top-right box) represent the kind of development required of each team member to grow and, collectively, create a high-performing team. I believe this is especially true the more senior the people.

I generally find that, overall, most teams don't collaborate naturally. This is because Dolphin-style attitudes require a purposeful shift in mindset. However, with practice, they can be easily learned – hence this chapter.

Most importantly, teams must deliberately commit to wiping out Fox-like behaviours. Such behaviours become divisive in the long term and ultimately lead to low-performing teams.

You can use the following exercises to help teams to develop those Dolphin-style attributes in a practical way.

## Collaboration assessment tool

On my website, you will find the 'Collaboration assessment' worksheet 3.2. As the facilitator, download and print it at A1 (flip chart) size for use by the team.

This assessment is done as a whole team (or initially in small groups and then discuss as a whole team). It provides teams with time for discussion and reflection. It self-creates an awareness of the importance of team collaboration based on the above Dolphin style.

The scoring is intended only as a subjective measure for the ensuing discussion.

## Collaboration principles – exercise

### Purpose

To take the learning from the 'Collaboration assessment' and agree to commit to a set of team collaboration principles (operating rules) that the team are willing to adhere to during all subsequent team meetings and discussions.

## Instructions

Talk through the Foxes, Dolphins, Baboons and Sheep model above.

Then, ask the team to go through and score the 'Collaboration assessment'.

Next spend time as a team collaborating, using all the Dolphin-style learnings from the exercise to create a set of principles that the team agrees to commit to.

As the facilitator, capture all agreed collaboration principles on a flip chart.

For larger groups, spilt into subgroups and allow time to feedback to the whole team and to agree actions.

## Reviewing actions

As the facilitator, it's important for you to spend time committing the team to deciding how and when they will apply, practise and adhere to the above principles over the next few weeks or months.

Type up a formal version and distribute as a team working document.

Remind the team of the importance of collaboration. Without this skill and quality you can't become a high-performing team.

Mention that a future team-building workshop could take this learning further by developing a team charter which will help them to consolidate these principles (*see* chapter, 'Have a team charter', later in this book).

The best feedback is what we don't want to hear.

George Raveling

# Use feedback

## Why is feedback important?

Feedback helps all of us understand ourselves better by becoming aware of how aspects of our behaviour can affect others. But most people, by default, hold back on giving feedback. Fear of entering a danger zone, letting the other person down or upsetting them are common reasons for this. However, high-performing teams understand the value of good feedback. Learning from it often makes all the difference to performance – because behaviour precedes results.

If you or other team mates are hesitant to give and receive feedback, you are not being honest with each other. In short, it breaks trust and the team ends up with reduced performance.

Feedback in teams helps individuals to be more aware of what they do and how they do it. Importantly, it also holds the whole team accountable for each other and makes them responsible for developing one another. In addition, it requires individuals to be honest and truthful with each other in terms of each other's strengths and weaknesses.

The process of feedback encourages everyone to learn to fine tune their behaviours so people and teams achieve outcomes and results. Furthermore, it helps teams and individuals enhance their credibility by eradicating or adjusting certain behaviours in a useful way.

The giving and receiving of feedback requires courage, tact, honesty, understanding and respect from both parties. It is also about naming certain behaviours in individuals but not attacking them as people or being spiteful. If done poorly, it can either be meaningless or create defensiveness and tension. When done well, the effects can be enormously beneficial.

## The Johari window model

The Johari window is a model used to help people and teams better understand their relationships among themselves and their interactions with others. It was created by psychologists Joseph Luft and Harrington Ingham in 1955. Their Johari window model was so named by them by combining their first names, Joe and Harry.

I suggest you copy this simple model onto a flip chart to introduce teams to the importance of feedback and why it is so useful.

Figure 5 Johari window

| | Known to self | | Not known to self |
|---|---|---|---|
| Known to others | Open | Known to others | Blindspot |
| Not known to others | Known to self | Not known to others | Not known to self |
| | Hidden | | Unknown potential |

The ultimate aim of the model is to show teams that good feedback can reduce a person's blind spot by helping them become more self-aware. In this way, feedback encourages individuals to open up and share more about themselves with others. Another pay-off is that it can increase a person's 'unknown potential' area, too.

## The importance of praise-based feedback in teams

Generally speaking, what happens to you if you hear the words, 'I'd like to give you some feedback'? The likelihood is that you've just felt your stomach clench strongly and you may have automatically thought: 'Oh dear, what have I done wrong?'

In my experience in the world of work, we rarely spend any time giving praise-based feedback. However, this is an important activity with which to create a high-performing team. Let me explain.

Many people associate feedback with personal weakness or something they've done wrong. So we brace ourselves to receive 'constructive' or 'developmental' feedback.

Conversely, when we're complimented in any way, we generally feel good about ourselves. However, it's a two-way street. You feel good all day having received it, but so will the person giving it. It is the same when we spend time genuinely praising or thanking someone for a job done well. It's a mutually beneficial process.

Therefore, learning to give genuine praise-based feedback freely in the work place and within teams is a very powerful way of building trusting interpersonal relationships. This is because people remember for a very long time – often for years – how they felt receiving it.

It's like playing tennis, when you strike the ball on the racket's 'sweet spot' and make a winning shot. The server of the shot feels good. But the receiver also acknowledges it as a great shot (as does the audience). Everybody wins.

However, you might be one of those people who reject a compliment through misplaced embarrassment or modesty. But it's important to remember that, by doing that, you also dismiss the courage it took for that person to pay you the compliment in the first place. Simply listening politely and saying thank you honours the other person in return.

## The compliments game – exercise

This praise-based exercise is very powerful, useful and enjoyable. I use it with teams that already know each other and have spent time working together in a workshop – say, as an ice-breaker to begin the second day of a workshop. Teams start off cautiously, but soon get into the spirit of it. People often report back that they loved doing it.

### Purpose

To help team members to get used to receiving and giving praised-based feedback. This exercise intentionally allows them to feel good about themselves. They get feedback about things they do well that they have not been told before. This builds strong confidence, trust and interpersonal relationships within a team.

### Instructions

Introduce the team to praise-based feedback and say why it's important. You can use the introduction given above under 'The importance of praise-based feedback in teams' heading.

Instruct team members to pair up and give each other a piece of praise-based feedback. Here's a script to help you along:

- Feedback must be genuine and based on a time when your partner did something well that also positively affected you in some way. Be as specific as you can. It could also be something general about their personality, behaviour or style that has been and continues to be helpful to you. Give reasons why you find this action or attribute helpful.

- If you are the recipient, listen carefully to and accept the feedback given to you. Say thank you when your partner has finished. Comment as you wish.

- Take it in turns, spending about 5–10 minutes or so on each feedback session, going back and forth conversationally.

- When a pair has finished and is ready to move on, form another pair with another team member who is also ready.

In this way, each person gives a piece of praised-based feedback to everyone else in the team.

## Practical points

Pairs should find a place to give their feedback – in the workshop room or elsewhere in the building or go for a short walk – where they can talk without being overheard.

If you are in the confines of a room, some gentle music can be played so the pairs cannot be easily overheard.

Generally, allow about two hours to complete this exercise, depending on the size of the team.

> ### Reviewing
>
> Ask for general feedback from the whole team about how they felt about the exercise, what was useful and what they learned overall.
>
> Remember that each conversation was private, so don't ask about specifics.

I have used this exercise with all sorts of levels, be it leadership, management or work-based.

One of the most important challenges of building a high-performance team is to be robust with each other and accountable to one another. This is particularly important for senior and leadership teams.

A powerful way of developing this is by being willing to overcome any hesitancy in giving one another constructive feedback. In the long run, failing to do this means that you will let each other down. By holding back, you will affect the whole team, too. In the end, it leads to low performance.

## Team feedback – exercise

### Purpose

For team members to provide each other with direct actionable feedback so that altering their individual behaviour can improve the performance of the team.

### Preparation

As the facilitator, give each team member a worksheet for them to complete in private as pre-work in advance of this session. (You can find an example of this on my website, worksheet 4.1.)

## Instructions

Referring to the pre-work, facilitate the group to take it in turns as a team to give positive feedback about some aspect of each person's valued behaviours.

Do the same for unhelpful aspects of the person's behaviour, which adversely impacts the team.

At the end of that, the person being fed back to responds.

As the facilitator, use a flip chart to record each person's valued and unhelpful behaviour feedback points.

When addressing aspects of unhelpful behaviour, remember to be honest and not hold back. Address the person's *behaviour* directly; don't attack them personally or be spiteful. This process is about being truthful with grace.

Do the same for each member of the team in turn.

As the facilitator, use a flip chart to record all of the strengths and weaknesses feedback for each person.

## Strengths and weaknesses – exercise

As feedback is so vital in the development of high-performing teams (particularly for senior staff), it is useful to do another round of feedback at a follow-up workshop sometime later. This exercise, which uses language based around strengths and weaknesses instead of behaviours, is designed to build further resilience.

As the facilitator, split the team into two groups. (For privacy, use two rooms.) Each group collectively completes the worksheet 4.2 (downloaded from my website) for each member in the other group. This template allows the team members to evaluate each other, listing the strengths and weaknesses of each individual.

Once complete, come together again as a whole team. Decide who is going to give feedback to whom. Take time as a whole group feeding back each person's strengths and weaknesses in turn. In this way everybody listens to each other's feedback, as you did with the previous exercise.

## Reviewing commitments

Ask each team member to commit personally to spending time reviewing the feedback on their own personal strengths and weaknesses and to report back on the strengths and weakness exercise at either the next team meeting or the next workshop.

To build further resilience with senior leadership teams, you can ask individual leaders whether they would commit to talking through their own feedback with their own teams that they manage (if applicable) within two weeks.

Commit team members to teach the benefits of Johari window to their own direct reports to further encourage a culture of openness across your organisation.

Remind the team that giving and receiving feedback is a vital skill and quality if they want to become a high-performing team.

Feedback comments can also be picked up individually in one-to-one coaching sessions.

# Develop a growth mindset

## Fixed mindset versus growth mindset

Becoming a high-performance team requires individuals to develop themselves. This becomes even more important at senior levels.

When you grow as an individual, you display openness, are seen as guided by virtues and appear to be focused on a positive mindset. In teams, it is shown by a belief in others and giving them a chance because you care about their success. As a result, people who feel supported within teams are motivated to do their very best work, which will contribute to high performance.

Developing personally also means raising your standards by operating with honesty and humility. That requires an inner change in individuals, which takes a bit of effort. This is a personal journey as much as a team one. It's about shedding poor behaviours and habits that inhibit personal growth. It's less about what you do, but all about maturing your character so that you become who you truly are and are meant to be.

Put simply, personal development is about going from a fixed mindset to a growth mindset – or moving from your vices to virtues.

To best explain how you can help a team to achieve this, it's useful for you to describe the following concepts and principles:

- Inner drives, vices and the 'shadow self'
- Leading with your virtues and growth values that help people to awaken their authentic self

## Inner drives

Richard Barrett, leadership and wellbeing author, eloquently suggests that powerful drives dominate the first part of our lives and early careers:

- The survival drive helps us to protect and defend ourselves.
- The social drive shapes our feelings and attitudes towards others and our relationships with them.
- The self-esteem and ego drive allows us strive to get what we want and desire.

Importantly, these drives form the basis of our personality style, how we tick and our attitudes to life. Through them, we begin to shape our early careers, too. But if we don't grow beyond them (as we are meant to), they eventually lead to a fixed mindset.

## Unmasking your 'shadow side'

According to the author Sandra Maitri, these drives are unfortunately also responsible for our limitations, habits, programmes, vices and shortfalls – what she calls the 'shadow side'. They are the 'baser' instincts of our shared humanity, and we all have them.

Figure 6 Instinctive drives, vices and the 'shadow side'

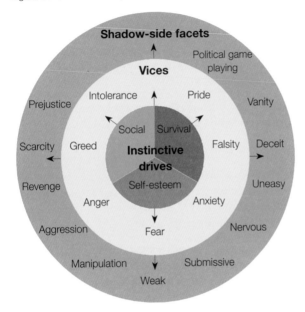

Our baser instinctive drives are at the middle of the graphic above. Working outward, these develop into our vices. Eventually they emerge as our shadow side.

The trick is for your personal development to grow beyond your shadow side and transform your character so that you become what you were always meant to become.

Left unchecked, our shadow side leads to low performance – e.g. manipulation, overcontrol, fear, dysfunction and ego. So, from a high-performance viewpoint, these are toxic traits and need ironing out.

However, it's not all bad news.

Counter-intuitively, your shadow side is also one of the building blocks for authentic leadership as you mature. By having the courage to tame your shadow side, you can learn valuable character-building lessons and consciously choose to make attitude adjustments along the way.

Leadership author Steven Snyder believes that, together, these struggles comprise the backstory that drives you.

## Awakening your authentic self

We all have an authentic self that calmly waits for the right moment and conditions to begin to nudge us subtly away from our shadow side and towards a growth mindset. Richard Barrett calls this the activation of the authentic self.

This gentle push is your authentic self, awakening. This is the 'transformation of self' phase. It's a natural part of maturing, but you must take note of it. Along with your backstory, developing a growth mindset unlocks leadership potential.

Have a look at the diagram on the next page. In individuals, the awakening of the authentic self starts from the centre circle.

Personal growth is about moving outwards towards developing your virtues. This takes conscious effort.

The outer circle represents what Richard Barrett describes as the growth values of:

- inner cohesion – finding meaning and togetherness
- making a difference in who we are and how we do what we do
- wider service – making the world better.

I believe that these growth values specifically apply to high-performing teams.

Figure 7 Authentic leadership growth values

**Backstories – exercise**

**Purpose**

To allow people to understand the concept of their shadow side. Valuable life lessons and growth lessons can be learned by overcoming this.

To understand that authenticity is not about *what* you do, but *who* you are and *how* you do what you do.

To reinforce the teachings we covered in the 'appreciative enquiry' exercise in the 'Build trust' chapter.

## Instructions

As the facilitator, introduce Figures 6 and 7 above to the team and ask for any observations. (You can download the text and diagrams from my website, 'Fixed mindset versus growth mindset' worksheet 5.1.)

In a relaxed and informal setting and using an 'appreciative inquiry' approach, ask team members to share with each other examples of their own backstory struggles or transformations.

If some of the team prefer only to listen to others talk through their experiences, that's fine. Don't put people under pressure.

Next, ask the group to discuss any 'light-bulb moments' and transformations, plus any lessons gained from those experiences that have built character and/or changed attitudes.

Draw out any specific learnings. For example, someone may have gone from vice to virtue. How did they do that – by mastering their ego, dealing with failure, battling through trials and trouble?

Finally, as a team, spend time reflecting on these backstories and discuss how you might apply such learnings as a team to move towards growth values.

## Notes

In my own experience, everyone identifies with this concept and so people engage readily with it. There will always be team members willing to share their personal journeys and others who enjoy listening to them and contribute later. I have found that those who are more senior generally have the maturity to handle this exercise and appreciate its value.

## Backstory examples

- I was a late developer, so school passed me by completely. It was only through work and a lecturer at my technical college who inspired me that my energies and passions were awakened. I discovered my drive to achieve, succeed and make a difference. However, I had to get over my own limiting belief that I was not good enough. I also had to work at overcoming my fears of not being liked and my anxiety (I'd had a stammer as a child) and my pride, all of which were powerful shadow-side drivers. In my mid-30s, I read Steven Covey's magnificent self-development book, *The Seven Habits of Highly Effective People*, and that was my transformation moment.

- An HR director I work with had recognised in her mid-20s that she'd been harbouring a limiting belief that 'All people are dangerous' – something that had developed during her formative years. In response, her shadow side had created the debilitating vices of anxiety and fear. Having worked on this issue at an earlier stage in her career, she has since transformed it into a virtue: 'People can be trusted.' That change resulted in a journey that took her from being a human resources officer to eventually end up as global HR director of one of the largest companies in the world. Today, her team benefit from her virtue of trust.

## Expanding team consciousness – exercise

This exercise takes further the examples above and at a team level. It is a powerful and practical process for a team to explore different styles of consciousness. It also encourages them to reach beyond basic instinctive drives and towards growth-based consciousness styles.

The exercise has been inspired and adapted for teams in the workplace from a concept called 'spiral dynamics' which I call 'styles of consciousness'. It also concurs with leadership expert, Richard Barrett, and his work on value driven organisations. In simple terms, it describes how each human group (including organisations) eventually forms a definable culture. Furthermore, each group culture can be generalised into one of eight stereotypical and recognisable styles of group consciousness. Each style is sequential, from one to eight. So, over time, each can evolve to the next level in the sequence.

For the purposes of this book, I only use six of these styles, the ones that best represent different organisational cultures. Each style of consciousness has different attributes and values and, for ease of use, each have been given a colour.

This approach helps all sorts of teams to better understand group culture and to learn more about themselves, their own team and organisational culture.

On my website you'll find the 'Styles of consciousness' worksheet 5.2 to download to carry out this exercise (as shown in Figure 8 on page 44). Make enough A4 copies to work with the team in groups.

## Purpose

To understand that consciousness evolves over time.

To help the team to understand that their consciousness forms a group culture.

To explore the ways that the team needs to develop to reach their full potential.

To discover who you are as individuals (and as a team) and what you stand for. This is just as important as the quality of the product or service you sell.

## Instructions

Split into small groups of three or four. A reasonable amount of floor space is needed to make this work.

Each group will be given six A4 paper copy of the 'Styles of consciousness' (containing six templates), each of which represents a style of consciousness. These can also represent different team or company cultures. A set of cultural attributes, language qualities and values that make up each style are listed on each of the six templates.

Ask each group to lay out on the floor all six A4 paper templates as shown in Figure 8 on the next page (but spread out in a line) and to follow these instructions:

1. Start by standing near styles 1, 2 and 3. Read the words in the circles and discuss any matches you recognise or observations you've made that might describe you as individuals, as a team or as a business (past or present). Notice that some of the qualities of each of the first three styles could be dysfunctional if overplayed.

2. Now move to styles 4, 5 and 6, repeating the first step. These styles represent higher levels of consciousness and a growth mindset.

3. Now return to the centre (between styles 3 and 4). Discuss all six styles and agree where each of you think you were, are and will be as individuals and as a team (and as an organisation) – in the past, now and next.

4. Come together as a group and take it in turn to report your observations to the rest of the team.

5. Help the team to find commonalities and agree on which style best represents the team: where they were, where they are now, and where they aspire to grow to next.

Figure 8 Six 'Styles of consciousness' summary

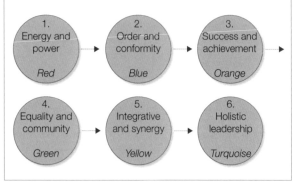

**Observations**

I have found that using the styles of consciousness with all sorts of different teams has additional pay-offs. Teams quickly begin to use language influenced from the 'Expanding team consciousness' exercise (particularly styles 4, 5 and 6 which depict a growth mindset).

Moreover, they quickly recognise the discordant nature of the basic instinctive styles (given in 1, 2 and 3), especially those qualities that are dysfunctional if overplayed.

One leadership team that I worked with successfully used the specific language qualities of styles 4 and 5 when presenting their annual budget review to their board. It had been an especially challenging year, sales-wise, for that company, but the team's work on the language used in their budget proposal struck a chord with the board who quickly approved it.

## Reviewing actions

Discuss the outputs from these exercises and specifically identify the practical benefits for the team.

Commit the team to subsequent actions to practise so they can move forward. Record these and distribute them later.

Remind the team that these are essential learnings to becoming a high-performance team and to personally grow into effective leaders.

Encourage the team to become aware of using more growth-based language with each other and in everyday communications and presentations.

Agree with the team when these activities will be revisited so that they can fine tune the principles learned. Often this will be on a later team-building day.

Individuals may wish to learn how to understand their shadow side on a more confidential basis, in which case one-to-one coaching would be appropriate.

But if thought corrupts language, language can also corrupt thought.

**George Orwell**

# Use purposeful language

In Abraham Maslow's well-known model – the 'hierarchy of needs' – he describes default basic needs that must be satisfied to reach self-actualisation: the pinnacle of high performance. This must be achieved through self-development.

That means that, to reach our own highest level of performance, we must move away from our default base instincts and develop ourselves towards our growth needs instead. This is what we began in the previous chapter, 'Develop a growth mindset'.

In this chapter, we will take this further. The exercises are designed to help team members become aware of the negative power of emotive language patterns. These exist as expressions not only in our conversations but more subtly as everyday thoughts, especially in negative inner mind chatter.

Working through these simple exercises as individuals and as a team is an effective motivator towards becoming a high-performing team.

As the facilitator, download the 'Use purposeful language' worksheet 6.1–6.4 from my website and make enough A4 copies for each person in the group. The exercises below are intended to be done in sequence one after another.

## Softening language – exercise

This exercise is a great starting point. It helps individuals to soften or moderate their own emotive language and to become more aware of others using it. It will also help team members gain more control over their feelings about the events, situations and circumstances they face in everyday business life.

It is also particularly useful for those individuals who tend to default very rapidly to states that are emotive, negative and forceful or find it hard to keep control over negative emotions.

### Purpose

To get the idea that softening or attenuating strongly emotive thoughts and feelings can dramatically reduce their impact on you and others. By reframing them, you can respond in a more self-controlled way. This helps teams get along and collaborate better.

### Instructions

Introduce the exercise using the explanation above to the group

Use worksheet 6.1, working in pairs, follow the instructions on the worksheet to change the emotive words into softer, 'less emotive' language tones.

To help people understand what's needed, some words have already been reframed.

Once the worksheet is complete, as a pair spend some time discussing how this activity can be applied as a team to enhance performance.

## Presupposing success

Did you know that what we presuppose in our inner thoughts and what we verbalise has tremendous power? This is because whatever you presuppose sets up what your attention will focus on and seek to fulfil.

*What you presuppose is a precondition of that happening.*

For example, every golf player quickly learns not to say or think: 'Don't hit the ball in the water.' That's because this sentence will predispose their nervous systems to perform in such a way that exactly that outcome results – and the ball ends up in the water.

We often hear 'Don't worry about...' this or that. But this type of language results in focusing our brain patterns on accessing that worry.

If you are insecure, nervous or anxious, your inner thought patterns and nervous system will be attuned to that. Therefore, you will tend to find that life throws up more and more things to be nervous or anxious about.

If you are an aggressive or angry person, then such thought patterns will set up the circumstances that provide you with reasons to defend yourself, lash out and be aggressive.

The saying 'Be careful what you wish for' certainly holds true.

Thinking about what you don't want sets up your attention to think about the very thing you don't want. If you think about the thing you don't want to happen, paradoxically it means that you end up getting the very think you wanted to avoid.

This is not an effective strategy and ultimately leads to low performance.

Breaking this pattern is important if you want to achieve high performance. By deliberately presupposing positive outcomes and success, both in inner thought patterns and in verbal communication, it will lead to better outcomes and results. In short, you get what you wanted instead.

Have a go at reframing the following presuppositions...

## Presupposing success – exercises

### Purpose

Negative thought patterns and language set up your attention to get what you don't want. Instead, using positive success-based thoughts and language patterns means you'll get the outcomes and effective results you want more often.

### Exercise 1: Presuppositions

As the facilitator, introduce this exercise with the preceding description. Have team members, working in pairs, transform the ineffective presuppositions into success-based, effective ones. Refer to worksheet 6.2 available on my website.

(Please see worksheet 6.3 on my website for the completed answers.)

### Exercise 2: NLP presuppositions

The presuppositions used in this next exercise are a set of ready-made success-based statements taken from Neuro Linguistic Programming (NLP). They are useful in helping to adjust our attitude to the world and to develop ourselves.

Here's an example: Respect the other person's model of the world.

Using worksheet 6.4 on my website ask the team to work as a whole group, or form subgroups and discuss the six ready-made presuppositions that you'll find there. The boxes on the worksheet are for any personal learnings to be noted.

It is important to remember that NLP doesn't claim that the statements are necessarily true – what's important is to try them out. If you act as if you believe that they are true, how would this change the way you perceive others and the world around you?

## Reviewing actions

- Ask each member of the team to commit to one or two of the exercise's presuppositions that they wish to 'try on' over the next few weeks, and notice what difference this makes to them. Many people I work with find these to be a game changer.

- Review 'Presupposing success' exercises 1 and 2 with the team. Discuss what they have learned about their own use of language and how employing success-based presuppositions might influence their interactions with others.

- Ask the team how the presuppositions could be applied to enhance personal and team performance. What we think and how we use language is one of the more subtle but crucial factors in becoming a highly effective successful team.

- One-to-one coaching for some team members may be a useful way of augmenting this work on language patterns.

Respect is the key determinant of high
performance. How much people respect
you determines how well they perform.

Brian Tracy

# Define values and behaviours

It is very useful for high-performing teams to spend time together establishing a set of enduring team values. A 'team value' is a concept that represents a motivating quality, priority or something important to you as a team.

From each team value, a subset of demonstrable behaviours can be agreed that represent specific actions or statements that the team then abide by. These are particularly helpful to refer to when clarifying day-to-day issues, dealing with conflict, and decision making. They also assist teams when calling each other to account due to poor behaviour.

Team values and their associated behaviours help to support high-performing teams to get the very best from one another.

## Team values and behaviours – exercise

### Purpose

To select team values and develop them into a set of agreed team behaviours that make them meaningful and actionable. By abiding by these behaviours, the team will operate at its best.

Both values and behaviours should be short and memorable.

## Instructions

As the facilitator, to carry out this exercise download the following worksheets:

The 'Styles of consciousness' worksheet 5.2. Make enough A4 copies to work with the team in groups of three or four. (This exercise was used in an earlier exercise in the chapter 'Develop a growth mindset'.)

The 'Team values and behaviours' worksheet 7.1. Print out at A1 (flip chart) size.

Spread out on the floor the six 'Styles of consciousness' templates in a line from one to six.

Choose four or five team values based on any of the words on the six 'Styles of consciousness' templates that you believe to be important to you as a group and to which you aspire. Feel free to adapt or choose different ones. (Remember that styles 4, 5 and 6 represent higher consciousness and team growth.)

Then, list the chosen team values on worksheet 7.1.

Come together as a team and share the selected team values. Collectively decide the team values that best describe what you desire to achieve as a team.

Next, as a whole team, work through the worksheet, completing each column in turn moving from left to right.

We will revisit this subject again in a later chapter on 'Have a team charter'.

## Behaviours drive culture

*This is the way things are done around here.*

If your workplace is given little leadership direction on behaviours and values, then its culture will end up shaping itself. Instead, a culture of unsaid, hidden codes of conduct will creep in to fill the vacuum. This will eventually form its own identity and will become unwritten rules. Unwritten rules tend to create problematic cultures.

Unwritten rules can often be found by unpacking this common phrase: 'This is the way things are done around here.'

Unwritten rules can be made worse by both managers and staff, simply by them shrugging their shoulders and putting up with them at all levels.

At first glance, there might seem nothing wrong with that. After all, what have unwritten rules got to do with business or profit? But ultimately unwritten rules drive behaviours, which in turn drive prevailing group cultures. These eventually translate into business results or a lack of them.

The thing is that poor behaviours – resulting from default, instinctive, fear-based thinking – quickly spread and end up becoming the norm, and so unwritten rules emerge and eventually root themselves deep in the company DNA. They are then hard to break. (We covered this in the 'Develop a growth mindset' chapter.)

The adage 'Old habits die hard' runs true.

This leads to all sorts of low-performance issues such as 'jobsworths', 'yes men', constant cost cutting, mean-spiritedness, overcontrol, workplace bullying, and a blame culture. For any company, that's a high price to pay.

High-performing leadership teams take a different approach. They take the time to purposefully form a great workplace culture that will satisfy the growth needs of their people. That in all likelihood will then yield sustained profits.

Part of this process is also to deliberately root out underlying unwritten rules and reframe them to encourage proactive and positive workplace behaviours instead.

## Proactive versus reactive behaviours – exercise

First talk through the above section on 'Behaviours drive culture' with the team and then use the following simple exercise as a starting point. It is best employed to help address behaviours that need challenging within the team. You can also use it as an ice-breaker alongside any other appropriate exercises in this book.

### Purpose

To become aware of underlying behaviours (or unwritten rules) within the team that diminish credibility.

To hold each other to account by calling out reactive behaviours and committing to using proactive behaviours.

### Instructions

Split the team into groups of about three or four and download the 'Proactive versus reactive behaviours' worksheet 7.2 from my website. Print it at A1 (flip chart) size.

*Start with reactive behaviours*

Thinking about you as a team, what three to four default reactive behaviour patterns (or unwritten rules) are you aware of that are unhelpful and diminish the credibility of your team?

Record each of these directly on the worksheet. Use Post-it® Notes and place them below the thick black line on the worksheet.

*Now turn your attention to proactive behaviours*

Thinking about you as a team, choose three or four new or existing proactive behaviour patterns that would be helpful in enhancing the credibility of your team and which you agree to commit to.

Record each of these on a Post-it® Note and place them above the thick black line on the same worksheet.

*Finally, share your findings with the whole team*

Agree to which of the under-the-line behaviours you will challenge whenever you experience them, and which of the above-the-line behaviours you will take forward as a team and commit to.

How will you keep this fresh in your team's collective mind so they will remain committed to it?

We will revisit this subject again in a later chapter on 'Have a team charter'.

## Transforming unwritten rules – exercise

This is an in-depth exercise.

Management teams, supervisors and team leaders will find it especially useful, to help them expose and transform any unwritten rules that may exist in their organisational culture. I have also used this with leadership teams, too. The exercise goes through a number of phases: exposing, transforming, consolidating, and committing to.

As the facilitator, I suggest that you talk through the earlier 'Behaviours drive culture' section above, so that your team will understand the principles and concepts behind unwritten rules and organisational culture and why it is important to expose and transform them.

It may take a while for your team to begin recognising these rules. So encourage them and tell them to take their time and they will begin to expose them.

Here are some real examples of unwritten rules. It may be helpful to give these to your team, so they don't have to start with the pressure of a blank sheet of paper. Do you recognise any of these rules in your team?

| | |
|---|---|
| Loudest person wins | Constantly moan about 'the management' |
| Us and them | |
| Not my job | No challenging of 'legacy' language |
| Blame others; not my fault | |
| Fear of failure, so don't speak up | Lack of challenge, feedback and recognition |
| Undermine other departments | Don't praise success enough |
| Tried before and didn't work | Don't spend time learning from failure |
| Paper over the cracks; don't spend time looking for the root cause | Let things fester |
| | Don't commit to decisions |
| Don't be different | Always being undermined |
| Focused in the past, no future outlook | Acceptable to miss deadlines |
| Don't support each other | Unclear about process, priorities and actions |

## Purpose

To expose the underlying unwritten rules that adversely affect organisational performance.

## Instructions

As the facilitator, download the 'Exposing unwritten rules' worksheets 7.3–7.6 from my website. Print out at A1 (flip chart) size.

Also download the 'Examples of real unwritten rules' worksheet 7.7 at A4 size.

Make enough copies so that there's one copy of all the worksheets for each group.

Split the team into groups of three or four people.

### Phase I – exploring unwritten rules (worksheet 7.3)

Working together, start to brainstorm the sorts of negative language and unwanted behaviours that you hear and observe in your organisation. Use Post-it® Notes or write directly on the worksheet to record your emerging thoughts.

### Phase II – defining unwritten rules (worksheet 7.4)

Taking the brainstorming work of the Phase I worksheet, now follow the instructions on the Phase II worksheet and turn them into phrases that represent simple unwritten rule statements. To help you, use the examples of 'real' unwritten rules above that were given to you.

Use Post-it® Notes or write on the worksheets.

All groups to feedback results of Phase II to whole team.

## Transforming new habits and behaviours

### Purpose

To transform each unwritten rule and its negative consequences by positive reframing that will promote performance improvement.

To commit the team to challenge and change the underlying
culture for the better.

### Instructions

*Phase III – transforming unwritten rules
(worksheet 7.5)*

Taking the output from Phase II working as a whole team,
agree on 5–8 habitual unwritten rule (UWR) statements that
most accurately represent the underlying culture. Record
these onto the Phase III worksheet.

Work on each unwritten rule one at a time. Moving from left
to right complete worksheet 7.5.

State the negative consequence of that rule on the culture.
Then reframe it. After that explore and state the positive
emotional impact of the reframe and the expected performance improvement.

*Phase IV – commitment statement sign off
(worksheet 7.6)*

Using the output from Phase III, create a commitment
statement that covers the points that you have all agreed
to change, adhere to and be accountable for, to create the
necessary shifts in organisational culture.

All team members should sign the statement.

We will revisit this subject again in the next chapter, 'Have a team charter'.

## Review actions

A superb supporting resource is Tim Gallwey's *The Inner Game of Work* (*see* Further reading).

Aspire greatly; anything less than a commitment to excellence becomes an acceptance of mediocrity.

Brian Tracy

# Have a team charter

A team charter is basically a written covenant, agreement or code of conduct that the team work together to create. It can consist of a set of values, habits and/or behaviours that the team are then willing to commit to, with each other and in their day-to-day work.

Creating a team charter pledges teams to high performance. I've found that it's worth spending time with teams – at all levels – to produce one. They can be a game changer for organisations subject to shifting cultures and unwritten rules.

A team charter needs to become part of the team's DNA in the following ways:

- Reminds the team of their core values and what they mean to them
- Drives behaviours for which the team will hold each other to account
- Identifies which reactive behaviours will be called out by the team
- Commits the team to a common purpose

The exercises used in the previous chapter are referred to again in this chapter.

## Do's and don'ts team charter – exercise

Here's a simple format that you can use with any team.

It is a further development of the 'Proactive versus reactive behaviours' exercise in the 'Define values and behaviours chapter' (see page 53). (If the team have previously done that exercise, then use it as a reference.)

Starting with a list of the company's core values, the team translates them into what each one represents or means to them. They then cascade down into commitment statements.

As the facilitator, download the 'Do's and don'ts team charter' worksheet 8.1 from my website. Print at A1 (flip chart) size and make enough copies for each subgroup.

### Purpose

To create a team charter based on core company values that the team will commit to and be accountable for.

### In advance of doing this exercise

Obtain your company's list of core values from your leadership team. (Most companies will have a list of core values.)

Shortlist the top five core values and add them across the top of the template. If you want to work with more than five core values then redraw the template to suit your needs. (I find less is more memorable.)

### Instructions

Split the team into groups of three or four.

Provide each group with a copy of the template with the core values already added, plus a set of Post-it® Notes.

Spend time working through the worksheet.

Then come together as a whole team for feedback and to draft a united team charter.

## Leadership team charter – exercise

This is more comprehensive than the previous exercise and designed for leadership teams. It will take time to complete.

As the facilitator, download the 'Leadership team charter' worksheet 8.2 from my website. It draws directly on the work completed in the 'Define values and behaviours' chapter.

### Instructions

You can do this exercise with the whole team (rather than in subgroups).

The 'Leadership team charter' worksheet is divided into three main segments. Complete each in turn as listed below:

*Top left segment*

Work as a team to complete the statements listed in the table.

This is an adaptation of a company's vision and mission statement, generally used to describe organisations. The top box approximately maps to 'vision' and the bottom box maps to 'mission'. I prefer this approach as it is more aligned and applicable to teams. For an alternative approach, see Richard Barrett's excellent work on vision and mission in his book *The New Leadership Paradigm* (*see* Further reading).

Don't rush this segment – it will take a while. I suggest you go through at least two iterations at separate team-building events.

*Top right segment*

This requires the team to first complete the 'Transforming unwritten rules' exercise described at the end of the previous chapter. (Phases I to III are required here only, not Phase IV).

Once the exercise is complete, then work as a team to turn the reframed rules into new behaviour commitment statements using the table provided on the 'Leadership team charter' worksheet.

*Bottom segment*

This requires the team to complete the 'Team values and behaviours' exercise (on page 53) described at the beginning of the previous chapter.

Add three or four relevant keywords that define you as a team. This is optional.

Signatures can be added as appropriate if the team wish to commit to the charter in this way and hold each other to account.

Spend as much time as necessary to review and agree on the text of each segment as you go through the exercise.

## True stories

### Story 1

For one team I worked with to develop their leadership team charter, it took two separate sessions to complete their first version. This became the pivotal outcome of their leadership development programme.

They then wanted to review it again as part of the agenda at two further team awaydays. Their diligence certainly paid off.

Once complete, their team charter was hung on the wall in their executive meeting room and became a set of principles that guided their conversations, debates and behaviours during all their meetings. Because of this, said the managing director, they quickly became a high-performing team. That's not all. The managing director also used the charter as a conversation piece whenever board directors and customers came to visit. This team became the exemplar of a high-performing team in their business community.

## Story 2

Another team I worked with used their leadership team charter (again developed over two sessions) to commit themselves to change the old habits and poor behaviours that had sapped morale and led to low performance. The creation of their charter caused a new energy and buzz for that team, which now began to work better together.

## Story 3

When an already high-performing team of outlet managing directors of a well-known regional restaurant used the 'Do's and Don'ts team charter' exercise, it helped them to define themselves. They wanted to identify in words what had created their success and their team spirit. This was then used to communicate what success looks like within the outlets they each were responsible for.

## Story 4

A marketing team I worked with used the 'Do's and Don'ts team charter' exercise and committed to display the results prominently on a wall of their team office. They also all signed it. When they later revisited this and made amendments, they added dated inked thumb prints to mark the occasion.

## Reviewing actions

The 'Leadership team charter' takes time to develop – as does each of its parts. It's important to put in the hours elaborating it, so don't rush the process. It is a serious piece of work.

Because of the importance of commitment in becoming a high-performing team, I recommend that, whatever version of the team charter you choose, you revisit it at subsequent team-building awaydays.

It's important, too, that you encourage the team to discuss how they will commit to their team charter, how they will hold each other to account and how they will ensure that the charter becomes part of the team's DNA. Also agree how the team's charter will be used to communicate downwards and upwards within the organisation.

Finally, discuss the ways it might impact positively on company culture.

# Plan creatively

Planning the future is an essential leadership activity. As the facilitator, you must follow an effective process to help teams plan ahead as well as ensuring that they are in the right frame of mind. Together, you will need to consider and debate all the different consequences that might impact the business.

These are examples of typical planning topics:

- Envisioning the future
- How to achieve big goals and ambitious targets
- Organisational restructures and changes
- Buyouts, mergers and acquisitions
- Exploring new markets
- Understanding the changing external landscape
- Competing against other organisations
- How to deal with critical company issues
- Appreciating how change will affect the company culture and its people

## The importance of creativity in planning

Exploring any complicated scenario will not be straightforward. Ask any general who has planned for a battle; they will tell you that such plans are made up of complexity and ambiguity. Business scenarios are no different. People's different viewpoints and multiple perspectives mean that there are no obvious right or wrong answers.

This is where creative thinking comes in. Using our imagination can very effectively help unblock thinking that has become stuck. But to get the most from our imaginative and creative sides, we need a process and some structure, too.

Here are some pointers to get the most from a planning session and achieve a successful outcome:

- A good planning process balances both structure and creative thinking. Yet, many people find thinking creatively a bit scary, or view it as being 'woolly' or 'fluffy'. However, when free-flowing creative thinking is deliberately introduced to a planning process, it will pay off. By allowing time and space for creative thinking, I guarantee that a team will dramatically exceed their own expectations.

- Make room for healthy debate and discussion. This will allow imaginative solutions and new agreements to emerge.

- Strategic planning must identify the primary high-level activities and actions required to deliver the strategy. These can then be worked up into logical and objective workstreams, along with more details, time scales, key resources and the budget pots needed to execute the strategy at a later point.

- Spend time considering and planning those things that are needed by internal and external stakeholders.

- Even more detailed project-based planning phases will be needed to execute the agreed actions and subsequent workstreams. This may include identifying appointments to manage the process and securing important resources and budgets.

## Seven keys to a successful strategic planning process

What makes an effective process?

1 It must be practical, creative, imaginative, collaborative and stretching. This is essential.

2 It must be enlightening, insightful and invigorating.

3 It must engage and motivate the whole team.

4 It must help the team achieve clarity from what initially seemed complex and ambiguous.

5 It must enable the team to be clear about their next steps.

6 It must provide tangible take-aways that the team can continue to work on and create projects and programmes from.

7 It must engender an appreciation of what's involved and the impacts and changes required in the future.

### The Big Think! – exercise

This is a three-phase practical and creative team process that starts by generating new ideas, choices, options, potentials and possibilities. These ideas then turn into a 'rich picture' format (a phrase created by Peter Checkland, see below). Finally, they transform again into an operational model of actions, manageable chunks and workstreams.

I call this approach 'The Big Think!' It is an engaging and motivating process that leadership, management and departmental teams enjoy doing and get a lot of benefit from.

It is adapted from 'soft systems' philosophy. Soft systems were developed back in the 1970s by Peter Checkland (*see* Further reading) as a way for managers to understand ambiguity and complexity when dealing with messy and unstructured problems and change. Inspired by Checkland's work, below I have created the process for teams.

Here's how to use it.

As the facilitator, download 'The Big Think!' worksheets 9.1–9.3 from my website. Print them out at A1 (flip chart) size and make enough copies for all the groups to work on.

Also print out the 'Completed examples information pack' worksheet 9.4 on A4 size. The groups will find this useful to refer to as they progress through each phase.

## Purpose

To take a complex, ambiguous strategic problem and, through a three-phased process, find clarity and agree a way forward, which can then be taken away, planned and executed.

## Pre-work – develop a scenario statement

Before the strategic planning day, spend time with the leader to develop one or more variations on a theme of a short, simple scenario based around an objective. A scenario will describe in one or two paragraphs the challenge, complexity and ambiguity to be explored and developed by the team on the planning day.

For large-scale change, it might be useful to consider the change from the following business viewpoints: markets and customers; products and solutions; people and culture; operations and finances.

## Instructions

Split the team into subgroups of three to five people and provide each group with the A1 worksheets and an A4 copy of the completed examples information pack for the team to refer to during each subsequent phase.

Each subgroup either works on the same scenario or on variations of the same theme.

### Phase I – Brainstorming analysis (worksheet 9.1)

In your subgroup, read the scenario–objective. Use the worksheet and the additional instructions you'll find on it to explore your initial thoughts, impressions, feelings and ideas, based on your subgroup's view of the scenario–objective and any other relevant information.

*This starts the creative process.*

### Phase II – Creating a rich picture (worksheet 9.2)

Using the output of Phase I, in your group, use the worksheet to create a 'rich picture' to express the scenario–objective. (Follow the additional instructions found on the worksheet.)

This is a collective visual representation of your Phase I work on what could be. A 'rich picture' creatively expresses the group's collective thoughts and observations in drawing form.

*This is the creative and imaginative part.*

### Feedback round

On completion of Phases I and II, get all the subgroups to feedback a summary of their work to the whole team. In this way, the team will start to understand wider contexts, differences and similarities.

#### *Phase III – Generating an operational model of the change (worksheet 9.3)*

Returning to the subgroups one final time, take the learnings from Phases I and II and turn your attention to how you might execute a high-level plan around the scenario–objective.

Use the worksheet on my website and follow the additional instructions found on it.

#### Notes

The input and output boxes summarise, respectively, the current situation, challenge or problem and the situation after the changes in the circles have been made.

The inner circle relates to direct activities and the outer circle to any additional influences from indirect sources, stakeholders, etc. The blank space outside the outer circle represents any relevant external or environmental factors.

Each high-level activity and action should be depicted in a bubble or box. Use connecting arrows to show the order of flow from one activity to another.

Once Phase III is complete, feedback all subgroup models to the whole team.

I have used this 'Big Think!' process with many leadership and management teams as well as functional teams. Here are a few examples of real-life scenarios that have been used to start the process. Notice how they are open and ambiguous statements:

- How can we add value by taking a 'customer feelings' approach in our chain of restaurant outlets?

- What 'best would look, feel and sound like' to drive our business forward and meet our business objectives over the next 18 months (and subsequent years).

- What is the single most important goal that we must achieve during an agreed period if we are to consider ourselves successful during that time? And what are the supporting objectives that must be accomplished to achieve that?

- As a senior management team: What's working well, what's difficult or challenging, not working so well, where do you want/desire to get to as a team? What are your key aspects and challenges to focus on in the near future?

## Reviewing actions

After 'The Big Think!' process is complete, ensure that the team spends time discussing the output from the models and collectively agree the high-level actions and workstreams involved in implementing whatever change programme (large or small) is required in the future. Models can be improved and adjusted to suit.

## Reporting out

It is important to spend time reporting out on the potential business and organisation impacts of any change. The format of this needs to align with the specific purpose, and so it is often useful to agree it ahead of time.

Here's a few real-life examples:

## Prepare a report out of

Top three points to make this a success. Feedback to the whole team.

This will be reported back to the main board for further discussion.

## Report out

At the end of this process, you will produce a set of attitudes and behaviours based on your core values that you will commit to and which will positively influence your customers' feelings.

A more structured approach 'Report out example' worksheet 9.4 can be found on my website. This summarises the potential impact of a change across an organisation and its core functions.

### Future sessions and communications

It is crucial too that you ensure that the team sets aside future dates to discuss implementation, resourcing, budgeting, recruiting and timescales of any subsequent change programme.

Make sure that the team considers producing a communication briefing or plan describing any future changes, their purposes, intentions and impacts on the business, stakeholders and employees.

# Team development programmes

## Worksheets

For most worksheets mentioned in this book, I arrange for these to be printed out on flip chart size (A1) from a local printer ahead of the team day. This makes them easily visible and are just the right size for group work.

All worksheets referred to in this book are available on my website (pdx-consulting.com/resources.htm). If you wish for any further information, please feel free to contact me.

## Acknowledging sources

All the tools and exercises in this book have been tried and tested by me. I have studied many of the works from notable experts in the field of leadership development, and have referred to them in this book. To these people I am grateful. Over time I have adapted and changed many of these and fine-tuned them to suit facilitating team development programmes.

We all stand on the shoulders of other experts that have gone before us. This is how knowledge is further refined. I hope you will do the same with this book, too. Whatever topic, exercise, tool or model I introduce to a team, I always start by referencing its source. This is right, proper and ethical: the source originator should always be acknowledged and honoured. It also gives credibility to the material you are about to use.

I often bring along the original books, too, so people can browse these and purchase their own copies if they are interested. I simply request that you do the same for this book.

### Additional resources

**Team assessment tool**: In the previous chapters 'Build trust' and 'Harness conflict', I refer to Patrick Lencioni's books on team dysfunctions. Lencioni has developed a great team assessment tool that can be used for any team of any size in any business.

The tool, which is online, helps by supplying teams with some objectively scored data to help them to analyse how they are doing, based on five categories: trust, openness to debate, commitment, accountability, and drive for results.

You can purchase online assessments from Lencioni's company, The Table Group: tablegroup.com/teamwork/online-team-assessment

**Personality profiling tools**: In the 'Build trust' chapter, I also referred to using personality profiling tools.

To become accredited to administrator one or more of these tools, refer to one or more of these links:

- MBTI®: opp.com/en/tools/MBTI
- TotalSDI: totalsdi.uk
- DiSC®: discassessment.co.uk

**Conflict profiling tool**: In the 'Harness conflict' chapter, I refer to Kenneth W Thomas's work on conflict in which he adds more detail to the Thomas-Kilmann model.

To augment teamwork on the subject of conflict, there is a useful conflict style assessment called the TKI conflict mode instrument: opp.com/en/tools/TKI This tool, which you can buy, helps individuals become aware of preferences for harnessing conflict. It is a very informative report, and I have occasionally found it useful with teams.

**Barrett's alternative approach**: In the middle of the chapter 'Develop a growth mindset', I included a concept called 'spiral dynamics' or 'styles of consciousness'. An alternative approach has been adopted by Richard Barrett's excellent research based on his seven levels of consciousness, which, in turn, was inspired by the work of Abraham Maslow. Barrett's concept is also useful to check out in his book *The New Leadership Paradigm* (*see* Further reading). His concept works well with teams, too. Barrett's company, Barrett Values Centre (valuescentre.com) is also a useful resource.

## Background reading for teams

I sometimes ask leadership teams to do some background reading ahead of facilitating them as a team. I have found this particularly useful with leadership team development programmes. It helps to set the scene and the tone of the programme in advance. You'll find my recommendations in Further reading.

For example, I have requested leaders read Patrick Lencioni's book, *The Five Dysfunctions of a Team*. It's a short and easy read in story form about a leadership team learning how to overcome dysfunction. At the back of the book is the team assessment tool that I mentioned above. So, along with reading the story, team members can manually complete the tool. They can then use this as context to begin facilitating their own team work.

Alternatively, another useful, easy, quick-to-read resource is Travis Bradberry's *Emotional Intelligence 2.0*, which will also give you access to a quick but comprehensive, complementary online questionnaire that measures emotional intelligence. High-performance teams and emotional intelligence go hand in hand, so Bradberry's work reinforces many of the exercises used in this book.

Either book can be referred to during team workshops and team development programmes.

## Team-building programmes

### Practical timing guidelines

While the chapters have been arranged in a logical order, many of the topics in this *Authority Guide* can be combined into any number of variations. However, what variation will work for you depends on what the scope and objectives are for the team with which you will be working and how much time you will have with them.

You can also combine the topics with other training and facilitation measures not covered in this book but which you have found useful.

To help you get started, I have included in this chapter some typical examples of successful team-building structures and timings.

## Stand-alone and mix-and-match topics

| Chapter | Exercise | Duration |
|---|---|---|
| Build trust | Foxes, Dolphins Baboons and Sheep intro | 30min |
| | Trust assessment review | 45min |
| | 'Stories from your past' exercise | 2–3hrs |
| | Personality profiling | 3hrs |
| | 'Components of trust' follow-up | 30min–1hr |
| | Review | 30min–1hr |
| Harness conflict | Background Relationship development model Conflict zones | 30min |
| | 'Depth frequency' exercise | 45min |
| | Conflict styles | 1hr 30min |
| | Review | 30min–1hr |
| Collaborate | Intro Foxes and Dolphins | 30min |
| | Collaboration principles | 1hr |
| | 'Commitment' exercise | 1hr |
| | Review | 30min–1hr |
| Use feedback | Background Johari window | 30min |
| | 'Praise-based feedback' intro 'Compliments' exercise | 2hrs 30min |

| Chapter | Exercise | Duration |
|---------|----------|----------|
| Use feedback | 'Team feedback' exercise | 2–3hrs |
| | Review | 30min–1hr |
| | 'Strengths and weaknesses' follow-up exercise | 3–3hrs 30min |
| Develop a growth mindset | Background | 30min |
| | 'Backstories' exercise | 2–3hrs |
| | 'Expanding team consciousness' exercise | 45min |
| | Core team values | 3hrs |
| Use purposeful language | 'Softening language' exercise Review | 45min |
| | 'Presupposing success language' exercise Review | 45min |
| | NLP presuppositions | 45min |
| | Action review | 30min |
| Define values and behaviours | Background | 30min |
| | 'Above- and below-the-line language' exercise Feedback | 1hr 30min |
| | 'Unwritten rules' exercise Commitment Action review | 4–5hrs |

# Have a team charter

*Do's and Don'ts team charter (half day)*

Access core company values ahead of time.

Time required from start to finish is around 2–3 hours.

*Leadership team charter (2 days)*

**Day 1**

Vision and Mission statement – allow 2 hours

'Expanding team consciousness' exercise (*see* previous table) – allow 45 minutes

Team values – allow around 3 hours

**Day 2**

'Unwritten rules' exercise (*see* previous table) – allow 4–5 hours

First review and commitments to use

*Separate follow-up (half or full day)*

Revisit team charter and adjust.

## Plan creatively

*'The Big Think!' (1 day)*

Introduction

Phases I–III

Report out

*Abridged version (half day)*

A shorter version of the above, using Phases I and II, followed by an action planning review, can be used to tease out smaller team objectives.

# Further reading

Baron, R. (2009) *The Enneagram Made Easy: Discover the nine types of people*. Harper One.

Barrett, R. (2011) *The New Leadership Paradigm*. Lulu.

Barrett, R. (2016) *A New Psychology of Human Well-being: An exploration of the influence of Ego-Soul Dynamics on mental and physical health*. Lulu.

Barrett, R. (2013) *The Values-Driven Organisation.* Routledge.

Beck, D.E. and Cowan, C. (2006) *Spiral Dynamics: Mastering values, leadership, and change (Exploring the New Science of Memetics)*. Blackwell.

Bradberry, T. (2009) *Emotional Intelligence 2.0.* SmartTalent.

Chapman, B. (2015) *Everybody Matters: The extraordinary power of caring for your people like family*. Penguin.

Checkland, P. (1990) *Soft Systems Methodology in Action*. Wiley.

Covey, S.R. (2004) *The Seven Habits of Highly Effective People.* Simon and Schuster.

'Enneagram of Personality'. Wikipedia. https://en.wikipedia.org/wiki/Enneagram_of_Personality Date accessed: Feb 2017

Gallwey, T. (1997) *The Inner Game of Work*. Villard Books.

Jenkins, A. (2014) *You Are More Than You Think: The return to your authentic self*. SRA Books.

'Johari window'. Wikipedia. https://en.wikipedia.org/wiki/Johari_window Date Accessed 2017

Laloux, F. (2014) *Reinventing Organizations: A guide to creating organizations inspired by the next stage in human consciousness*. Nelson Parker.

Lencioni, P. (2005) *Overcoming the Five Dysfunctions of a Team: A field guide for leaders, managers, and facilitators*. John Wiley & Sons.

Lencioni, P. (2011) *The Five Dysfunctions of a Team: A leadership fable*. Enhanced edition. Jossey-Bass.

Maitri, S. (2000) *The Spiritual Dimension of the Enneagram: Nine faces of the soul*. TarcherPerigee.

Robbins, T. (2001) *Awaken the Giant Within: How to take immediate control of your mental, emotional, physical and financial life*. Pocket Books.

Snyder, S. (2013) *Leadership and the Art of Struggle*. Berrett-Koehler.

Thomas, K.W. (2002) *Introduction to Conflict Management*. CPP.

# About the author

Andrew Jenkins is a leadership development consultant and a dynamic, skilled facilitator, presenter and teacher of new thinking. He is the managing director of PDx Consulting Ltd, a consultancy dedicated to developing leaders, managers and executives so that their thinking is enriched and they perform at their very best. In addition, Andrew speaks, writes and blogs about new ways of thinking, leading and being.

It is Andrew's belief that macro-economics will continue to radically change employment, demographics, wealth distribution and job security. Old-world jobs are being swept away and new opportunities are emerging to build new-world economies.

In this new, rising global economy, executives will need to be significantly more supported and encouraged so they can reach their full potential and best use their talents and creative abilities at work. To meet these challenges and seize the opportunities that lie ahead, senior people at all levels will need to learn how to connect much more emotionally to one another and to their teams to facilitate these sorts of transformations.

In the new global economy, people will be regularly changing careers and continually learning and honing new entrepreneurial mindsets. So we will all need to learn to adapt quickly to change, bring our very best selves to work and be at the 'top of our game' during our varied and multi-faceted careers.

According to Andrew, we are all striving to find a sense of purpose and be fulfilled – whistling on the way into work in the morning and singing on the way home once work is done. This is the purpose and philosophy behind Andrew's approach to leadership development.

G000255081

Gallery Books
*Editor* Peter Fallon
HAPPY HOUR

Andrew Jamison

# HAPPY HOUR

For Deborah,

Very best wishes,

Andrew Jamison

25/3/13

Gallery Books

*Happy Hour*
is first published
simultaneously in paperback
and in a clothbound edition
on 2 July 2012.

The Gallery Press
Loughcrew
Oldcastle
County Meath
Ireland

www.gallerypress.com

*All rights reserved. For permission
to reprint or broadcast these poems,
write to The Gallery Press.*

© Andrew Jamison 2012

ISBN 978 1 85235 532 6 *paperback*
     978 1 85235 533 3 *clothbound*

A CIP catalogue record for this book
is available from the British Library.

the arts council schomhairle ealaíon | funding literature | artscouncil.ie

# Contents

*for David Park*

## The Bus to Belfast

An unstubbed cigarette butt — I can picture it now —
will be smouldering at the door of Toal's.
Between the Mace and Carman's Inn opposite
the chapel I'll lean on the lamp-post bus stop.
The Ulsterbus will slink down the hill
into Crossgar on the first Thursday after Christmas.
The hydraulic door will huff open. I'll step in.

The tenner I tender will elicit an epic *tut*
from the part-time bodybuilder driver,
raising the plucked eyebrows on his sunbed-seared mug.
There'll be a hair gel smudge on the window by my seat.
The pane's black rubber seal will be nicked to bits
by a penknife. The backs of seats will be plastered
in permanent pen signatures, initialled hearts,

and patches singed by cigarette lighters;
chewing gum and misspelt taunts in Tippex.
December sky will dazzle Carryduff. A flash of sun
will flare first, then flicker for a while through my eyes
as we hurtle past Pizza Hut, Winemark, then the Spar.
We'll shuffle by Forestside. Nothing will have changed.
That house over the graveyard will still be up for sale.

## The Curzon

And when the credits rolled and lights went up
the ceiling seemed unreachable as sky.
On either side of us was hung an ocean
of curtained wall. And yet the building seemed
so small, so humble from without
as if itself some sort of optical illusion,
some special effect, a trick of the eye
that got us every time. And there we are:

I see us now, my mother and my sister and myself,
late-ish, last minute for a matinee perhaps,
all greeted by a darkened room and backs of heads,
steady as we go along the LED-lined floor —
each aisle a dotted runway strip
as seats are taken, lights dimmed, minds blown.

## Listening to Ash

Hardly Mozart but I can't beat it,
can't knock these tunes that take me back, track after track,
wherever I am (Dalston, Glasgow, Fife)
to this road and that lay-by and every ditch
and field that line the way to Killyleagh
and it's 'Girl from Mars', 'Goldfinger',
'A Life Less Ordinary' and 'Uncle Pat'
and 'Jesus Says', 'Kung Fu', 'Oh Yeah' and 'Shining Light'.

And there I am, on the bus heading home from school,
and there's the telephone exchange, Mullan's bar,
the cricket club and then the Quoile, its greenery,
the swampy underpass that is the river
running through the bridge, the bridge, there's the old bridge.
Adolescence summed and summoned up by a riff.

## Afternoon

I knew the afternoon was coming to a close —
and it's alright that you weren't there with me —
as I made out a star from my window.
But that was fine. There is no afternoon
that can go on forever, no sky permanently orange;
no plane hangs in the air halfway to wherever,
no jet stream and no cloud eludes the laws of water,
no smoke rejoins the first flame of the fire,
no tree with no leaf that falls over and over
through a world where it is always afternoon.
Afternoon — the word itself is easy on the ear
full of soft *f* and those, those slowed up *os*
that melt away to nothing on the tongue.
We love it because it leaves us, becomes evening.

## Valerie

You'd been asleep and missed the tea and coffee cart.
Through the carriage it was all sunlight and quiet

(I'd been rubbing the sleep out of my eyes)
as both of us missed the minute's silence

that Sunday morning. Glasgow to Edinburgh.
And you were wearing what I took for a pashmina;

breathtaking, while wreaths were laid round cenotaphs
at Passchendaele, Marseilles, Nice, Nantes, Ypres.

## This Whole Place

There is nostalgia deep in the very bolts
of these steel seats outside the Europa bus station
which, here, this evening, sit me down and make me face
the evening, face to face and bus by bus,
as bus by bus sunlight falls out of love with Cavehill
and leaves me here nostalgic, wondering
what there is to love and what nostalgia's all about.

And there is disappointment deep
in the mayonnaise of my chicken sandwich,
my return ticket, the holes which are developing
all through my jeans and Converse, the sigh
that comes with sitting down which, also, is developing
as disappointment and nostalgia spray-paint themselves
onto this journey home; which is itself a city

in a way. And there is melancholy too,
deep in the come-and-go of this whole place
behind the laughter in the pubs and parks
and in the rush to cross the road and open doors.
And everywhere is everything. And nothing
comes but every way that nothing can.
And by 'this whole place' I don't just mean Belfast.

## Chancer

Although I can't fill out a betting slip,
don't know a spread bet from a buttery spread,
can't tell a furlong from a long fur coat,
the difference in a syndicate and Dick Van Dyke,
can't see the point to a point-to-point,
don't study tabloid pullouts or *The Racing Post*,
or check the form or follow a favourite jockey,
don't care about the half-past-five at Aintree
or Cheltenham on Channel 4 or Sky TV;
so, although I can't fill out a betting slip
(those fractions and odds are beyond me),
I, in my own way, am a gambling man:
I'm putting pen to paper, here and now,
and hoping to God the going is good.

# Death's Door

*after Jorge Guillen*

I have been mulling it over,
this now-and-again they call the future.
Because it comes to me: this door, ajar,

a chink that lights up some corridor
through the last house, last street, last quarter
of some lost city. It is a silent corner.

Someone, remind me it is summer,
this — a gin and tonic, each finger
already numbing round the tumbler.

## The Starlings

Everything, relatively speaking,
is simple: a tree a tree, the sky the sky,

the clock on the wall the clock on the wall,
a tick a tick, a tock a tock, time time.

And then come the starlings, tearing about,
beautiful obliterations of the commonplace,

going through the motions
of their unchoreographed airshow,

tremendously alike,
tremendously alone.

# How Was New York?

Contentment was a walk in the shade of the trees
on Staten Island, a Hudson breeze.

Sunburn meant getting lost for hours in Greenwich
Village, satisfaction a refrigerated peach.

Disappointment the mouse droppings around the sink,
the broken toilet, the oven on the blink.

Regret was the girl beside me on the subway,
sex the Village chicks who had it all on display.

Ambition was the young man's polished loafers,
hope the busker's outstretched cap, its rattling quarters.

Spirit was the kid selling ice-cold water
out of a bucket outside the Yankees game — a bottle a dollar.

Fame was impossible as the sound of the moon,
tragedy the elephant in the room.

Freedom was strolling up Bedford Avenue,
hate the heat. Impossibility — the sky's blue.

Forgiveness was the air-conditioner,
redemption all-you-can-eat moules-frites for dinner.

Near Brooklyn Bridge I found extravagance.
At Cadman Plaza war, limestone, remembrance.

Chaos was a dash over Queensboro Bridge at rush hour,
weird the earthquake's 5.8 on the Richter.

Surprise my rooftop fire escape's Manhattan,
Manhattan a hot dog stand, a metro map, a plan.

Goodbye was Newark airport in the evening,
grief the runway's lights, time zones changing.

## New York Minutes

Flowers on the walls, sunlight on the trees.
August. Friday afternoon. 49th Street. Queens.
Two vacant chairs outside Café Marlene —
half five, it seems, is not the time for coffee.
Car horns are honked like fuck, fire escapes
are bored: so much heat and not a flame.
Out of earshot and eyesight the 7 train —
rush hour — stops and starts its way to Manhattan,
to Grand Central — palatial in the hecticness.
On the observation deck of the Empire State
a family has that all-day sightseeing look —
with the world at their feet, all they want's the hotel.
Two honeymooners take the 3-hour Circle Line Tour,
loving every second. A stranger takes their photo.

## I Wanna Be a Part of It

There's no bacon in the bacon,
only sugar in the orange juice;
tap water makes me thirstier;
the fan can only circulate the heat;
the toaster doesn't work
and the kettle is about to blow;
so many streets and avenues and boulevards
but which way are you meant to go?
The cashier says, 'have a nice day',
but she's taken almost all my money.

# Listening to Kings of Convenience

In the arpeggioed, folky early stuff
like 'Toxic Girl' the bass drum's *dumph-dumph-dumph*

which signals the lead solo stands out a mile,
the timing of it almost as comical

as the *dink-dink-dink* of the opening harmonic —
somewhere between idyllic and ironic —

and the bassline saunters, *bum-bum*s along,
like all good basslines, only noticed when they're gone.

## Thinking of You on an Evening Walk in January

Tonight there were lights on the other hill,
the pavement glittered ice, middle-aged women
ran in breathable, high vis, streamlined sportswear,
snatching breath between snatches of conversation,
the cash machines blinked; there was nobody
at the bus stops, even the supermarket car park
was empty, there was the moon of course,
a star or two, and there were planes in the sky —
some taking off, some touching down — trees were bare,
curtains were open to well-lit living rooms
where the obligatory plasma hung on the wall,
nine-to-fivers, worked to the bone, slumped on the couch,
taxi drivers waited by the side of the road
under streetlights that flickered and burned and buzzed.

# The Early Hours

*after Manuel Bandeira*

What are we to make
of the sick at heart, up late,
dithering over each
and every unkissed kiss?

Such a song and dance
is made in these, the early hours,
full of shipping forecasts
and emptied bars.

Go down by the shore:
nightwalkers are done for.
They've had enough.
The tide has been too much like love.

Night-blooming cereus,
what are you to make of us?

## Orpheus

They said that when he played the sun would rise
in the east. But I can't be sure about all this.

And so I sit in mid-November, unconvinced,
which is to say, in need of some convincing

that there's a song, arpeggio, a riff,
to turn the world away from all these night-full days

which fill themselves with fallen leaves,
and the wistful, fallen version of ourselves.

So, Orpheus, here is the benefit of the doubt:
give us one for the road,

put a song in our hearts, play us out.

# Eating Alone in an Empty Diner

There's nothing romantic about it,
eating alone in an empty diner;
there's nothing healthy about it either,
ordering the burger with American cheese
(which isn't cheese at all) and the Coke
and the deep-fat-fried-from-frozen fries;
there's really nothing new about any of this:
the highly strung, chatty New Yorkettes that pass
with those silly little fluffballs, hairballs for dogs
which everyone seems to admire but me,
and iced coffee which everyone's drinking but me,
wearing shorts which everyone's wearing but me,
and flip-flops which everyone's flipping
and flopping up and down and around in but me,
so maybe that explains it all — I've thought — me sitting there
eating alone in an empty diner
on Houston Street near Washington Square,
asking the waiter to repeat himself,
away from wherever everyone else was,
getting to the ice-cube-water finish of my drink,
handed the change and handing back the tip,
somewhere near the end of happy hour.

## Subway Poem

Hot as hell. Black as hell. Fast as hell.
Crammed as hell. Sweating like hell. Awkward
as hell. Confusing as hell. Delayed
as hell. Uncomfortable as hell. Sexy
as hell. Is she smiling at you? Like hell.
Fat as hell. Smelling like hell. Her legs
are as long as hell. Her bust is as big as hell.
His bust is as big as hell. Braking like hell.
Piling in like hell. Looking like hell.
Reading like hell. Sleeping like hell. Kissing
like hell. Drinking like hell. Drunk as hell.
Sad as hell. Beautiful as hell. Noisy as hell. What the hell.
Hungry as hell. Tired as hell. Thirsty as hell.
Texting like hell. Laughing like hell. Quiet as hell.
Thinking like hell. Checking the time like hell.

## Sleepless in the Big Apple

Wired up on a large late-night latte
    and bottles of Sam Adams *Boston Ale*
with tomorrow fast becoming today —
    I've listened to Feist on repeat — 'I Feel it All'

but hear above it the 7 train
    making its way up Roosevelt Avenue,
its tooted horn like a discordant refrain
    or first sax note of a jazz tune, kind of blue.

## Autumning

There's bound to be something in this, this autumning
of August, this unsummering of the garden,
and the sky that meant so much to the garden
when it was blue with all those birds, those birds
you've never seen before so take a double-take for,
that leave you saying 'look at that' or nothing at all.
For now, although there's drizzle, there's colour,
there's colour in the gardenered hedgerows —
all carefully arranged and clashless,
full of dinner-table-poseyable flowers —
and in each ungardenered, blink-and-you'll-miss-it ditch,
gorse flowers preside as their own kind of light.
And as sunlight, with all its little nostalgia,
touches, or has touched, for the last time
someone's faraway field or scope of sea,
bookshelf, backyard, doorstep or bedroom wall,
so autumn comes like summer's broken promise
and nothing lasts, again: not the ink in the pen,
not the bulb in the lamp, not the glass in the window,
not the sky in the sky, not the flower in the flower,
not even this rain we never asked for.

# Sunnybank Avenue

*for Joe Loudon and Jonathan Travis*

I've got a lot of time for this time of night,
after after-dinner, before the falling out

of the world with the dark — which is to say morning —
before the falling over, tumbling, cavorting

of all consciousness — which is to say sleep —
daylight as yet a promise the sun might keep,

which is really just a fancy way of saying
the future, tomorrow, nothing is staying.

## King's Cross to Leeds

The train will soon depart
and soon a sinking of the heart
begin as everything
goes through a northerning:

relinquishing the south
the night opens her mouth
as some read *Metro* headlines,
some text, some close their eyes.

What love is given up
between each station's stop?
How many dreams died out
beneath each passed streetlight?

## Bigger Picture

Opened-window evening air keeps me awake
through another bout of lesson planning,
another struggle with objectives, outcomes
and all the other terminologies
shoved down the trainee's neck, term after term,
interminably. Somewhere a sun is setting,
a sea is falling over itself to reach a shore,
a sky is darkening only to set a city alight
as here tomorrow darkens the door.
Does Day have a *focus* or a *target*
which is *measurable, achievable,*
is it bearing in mind the *bigger picture*?
And when Night is all stars and moonlight
is this *good, satisfactory* or *inadequate*?

# BALLS

To drive a golf ball into Strangford Lough
is not to care if it's a fade, a draw, a hook or slice,
is not to care that hooking is the same as drawing,
is not to care that slicing is the same as fading,
is not to care for words in general;
to smack a golf ball into Strangford Lough
is not to care about the pin, the green,
the fairway and the rough, is not to count the score;
to absolutely hammer a *Slazenger*
into some expanse of open water
is to reconnect with something instinctive, primal:
to hit, as far as possible, anything spherical;
it is to be pissed off, frustrated, to nail,
contemptibly, a *Titleist* hundreds of yards
into the shimmer of a Sunday morning's Strangford Lough;
but it gets you nowhere, it is to pollute
its ancient floor forever, it is to waste
your energy, your time and money
to unforgivingly throttle a *Pinnacle*
into the watery winds of Down; it is not beautiful
and does not represent the endless pain of man
or death, it is a drop in the ocean
to have pasted, belted, whacked, thumped, clattered, blasted,
to have pinged, pranged, zinged, whammied, walloped, clanged,
sizzled, smashed a *Maxfli* into Strangford Lough
and the eye-blinding glister of an October a.m.
ten shots over par after the third hole on Mahee Island,
undeniably, irrefutably,
indisputably, is to have lost it.

# Killyleagh Road at Night in Snow

*after Pablo Neruda*

This should be the hour of fallen leaves
but is instead the hour of fallen snow.
I ponder old predicaments:
when there are words there seldom is a pen;
when there's a pen the words are seldom there.

Anonymous birds have scurried through the garden,
the moon has been observed for far too long
and nothing has been done because nothing
is urgent in the snow. The earth in snow
has slowed and shown her necessariness
and solitude has found a friend in night

but this should be the hour of fallen leaves.

## Winter Clearance

Weekend sales run into Monday, Tuesday,
unwanted clothes are cast to the floor
or over mannequins or other clothes
or sales assistants or small, unseen children.
No one can wait. Queues snake out doors, down streets,
the changing rooms are occupied, and anyway
they will not have that item in that size.
No one can find what they are looking for.

# Baucis and Philemon

*i.m. Joe and Martha*

They could have been Baucis and Philemon,
my grandparents in another life,
but not the lovey-dovey kissy-kissy version
we've come to know of that mythical man and wife.

She would have said: 'Joe, fill the coal bucket
and put on a fire for these here two callers.
Away you go.' And he, turning, would retort:
'All right, woman. Hol' on to your knickers.

'You can put the kettle on and wet the tea
and our visitors here might like a biscuit.'
'You sing and I'll dance,' she'll reply, all too ready
for this game of affectionate backchat.

And then they would become two trees forever,
but not like in the lovey-dovey kissy-kissy version.
I imagine them tangled ('Move over.' '*You* move over.'),
keeping each other going, carrying on.

# Old Man Autumn

Sombre and slow, ratchety, cranky and glum:
this is the geriatric sun of autumn;

knackered, it leans on leafless trees,
or dozes, before it disappears, over the eaves;

zimmer-framing, steady as it goes, through November,
it will leave us in the dark and take forever.

# Transatlantic

Outside: the throng of a typical Saturday afternoon in Leeds.
It is October. There is sunlight. There is the type of sunlight
that is particular to October. Gutters shine with it.
On the Headrow daytime drinkers step out into it for a puff,
then back away from it, just in time for kick-off on the big
    screen,
fingering the betting slips in their pockets. It is that time of day.

An obvious time of day, in many ways. Nothing is surprising.
Boyfriend and girlfriend shopping. Students getting home
    from last night.
The paranoia that comes with a come-down or severe hangover
is seen in those who hunch their shoulders, avoid eye contact.
Teenage girls bear too much skin and hang their handbags
from their upturned wrist. Teenage boys have gaping holes in
    their earlobes.
There are those who scroll their BlackBerry,
those who wear the white headphones of an iPhone or iPod,
intent on keeping in touch.

In New York it's only morning.
Subways in Queens are *over*ground,
with the Empire State Building in sight.
The 7 train makes a sound
too musical to be a honk
as it moves through 52nd to 46th
from Roosevelt Ave.

The red security shutter on a wine bar on Skillman
is still down, revealing some half-washed-away,
half-legible graffiti. There are no lights on in the Irish bars.
A Circle Line boat leaves for its first tour of the day.
Museums open. Lines accumulate. It is October there too.

Clothes hang on fire escapes. Early risers walk around
with cardboard coffee cups. The sky is a high blue.
Runners, finished, linger outside their apartments
with their hands on their hips and tilt their heads back,
grimacing up into the sky. Some turn on the radio,
open the window, slug from a large carton of milk,
then fry streaky bacon.

In Brooklyn the trees are losing their leaves.
Post drops on doormats in the palatial hallways
that line Columbia Heights. An old man,
in a dressing gown and trainers, unwashed, unshaven,
opens his front door, sits on the steps with *The New York
    Times*
and smokes a large, expensive-looking cigar.

A young male tourist is looking for the house
where his favourite writer used to live. A madman
sits on a bench, on the walkway above Brooklyn Expressway
and watches the helicopters circle. Two skater-kids rattle
    along.
A girl wears large shades, a flowery dress and pumps;
she stops, sits, talks on the phone to her boyfriend.
A passerby falls in love with her.
The East River runs into the Hudson.

## What I'll Say When I Get Back

This is the place, I'll say, no one and nothing
but a two-seat bench I'll sit on by myself
(because I will have come alone) and only the sound
of the river (which could be the Aire) behind my back,
the fields folding out to something like a town
beyond, and there's the path that brought me here
replete with dog turd and sheep shit and rocks
and puddles and muck which will take me back,
if I like, under the streetlights which won't yet be lit,
past the manicurist and used-car garage,
and then the all familiar turn-in to my avenue,
to my back door, the empty wine and beer bottles
I must get round to recycling, missed calls
I should return. But if I'll hold on
I'll see the path goes on and is the path
I might yet take, leading as it does
past the last pylons and last of the kept horses,
to more of the sound of more of the river.

## At the End of the Day

When all the cups of tea are drunk, dinners done,
correspondents left uncorresponded,
the all-encompassing silence of ourselves
is amplified as we, loud-mouthed, return
to our respective rooms, respectable
when the curtains are closed, blinds shuttered
against the prying eyes of country darkness,
the strange behaviour of unnameable birds,
the constant imposition of sky and grass
and all the nosiness of moons and stars.
Well, this is where we practise solitude:
'Remember when so and so said such and such
about this and that' — talking to ourselves,
getting over things, in a world of our own.

## Summer's Time

The sky is inoffensive, easy on the eye,
as stock is taken, the day's first rain watched,

or rather noted, or rather unimagined
over the marauding, inquisitive heifers

and bullocks in the field which take their time
as swallows take up their grudge with gravity,

as I begrudge the moment its prerogative
to come and go, to up and leave, to please

and help itself, to go about its business
as if without a thought or care in the world.

# Listening to Them

As Van gets stuck in to 'Baby Please Don't Go'
after the *bu-dum bu-dum* bass intro

after the lead guitar kicking off, kicking in,
doing a jingly jangly wild-western thing

I've tried to play on my Epiphone acoustic,
I think over each single, solitary lyric:

*Baby please don't go, baby please don't go*
*down to New Orleans, you know I love you so.*

## Twelfth

The stacked pallets of an unlit bonfire
in a Ballynahinch supermarket car park
on a piss of a day near the Twelfth of July,
looked down upon by the hills of Dromore,
circled by kids having races, doing wheelies,
in the summer of the summer of their lives,
come back even now, as I picture it all
however many summers later,
can see the chippy vans across the country
wheeled out, washed down, scrubbed up and gutted
to feed the Orangemen on burgers and onions
in the demonstration fields where a man will speak,
demonstrably, on a dodgy PA system
from the back of an open-sided lorry
about God and Ulster and God again
before a mock King Billy will appear
all dressed up and doing a kind of dressage
on one of those white horses that's seen better days,
as youngsters — beetroot, puff-cheeked — beat the life
clean out of their miniature Lambeg drums.

## Meditation on Ikea

In a world of cut-price faux-pine flat-pack,
of Allen keys and step-by-step manuals,
of straight-laced straight-faced Scandinavian design,
chairs churned out by the second in some far-flung factory
and sold by the lorry-load in big blue bags
in big blue warehouses at the express-
all-major-credit-cards-accepted self-service checkout
beside the in-store grab-and-go dine-and-dash
snooze-and-lose hurry-up-and-queue café
which serves the flash-fried speciality meatballs
next-door to the one-way three-tiered multi-storey
lifts-serving-all-floors pay-and-go car park
by the slip-lane of the new-improved motorway
down from the one-in one-out traffic-controlled airport
under the come-and-go clouds of an ever-changeable sky
and under all those burning stars, suns, systems.

# Thinking about the Point of Things

Sunlight shows up the dirt on the window —
bird shit, streaks of rain-stain from an overnight shower
put the pristine white of the PVC frame to shame —
a Belfast-bound flight disappears into Belfast,
flares and unflares in the soft blaze of a spring evening
like a second sun, or a one-off star
through this one-off, belter of a blue sky,
as it's radioed through its last approach
touching down to a province of 'politics' —
we'd call it something else if there was a word for it —
untouched by the in-your-face canvassing,
the prospect of door-to-door campaigning,
the lecturing in the electioneering
that's going on and is ongoing now
as lamp posts wear placards of touched-up,
photoshopped, yet puffy, pasty-faced politicians,
cable tied, fastened to streetlight after streetlight
by some fastidious, unpaid recruit, with hope:
busybodies, do-gooders who've got done over.
MEPs' double chins belie their à la carte lifestyles —
scream 'foie gras to start, fillet steak, then the cheeseboard';
a taxing regime of lunches on tick to the taxpayer —
there they are, beside words like *future, your, vote, for,*
the same old same old from the same old-timers
while buccaneery young bucks bear the look of the duped;
dimpled, malevolent grins of hardliners,
the streets of Crossgar are festooned with them,
wherever you look — left, right and centre —
like a festival without the festivities,
festivities without a festival,
or come to think of it, a festival without a festival,
but their greens and their blues will fester and fade
in the elements, the heat and the rain that will fall
through all the Baltic founderings of an Ulster winter,
rare days of summer's sun-split trees, heat-woven lull,

as lampooners, gossipers, small talkers
lampoon, gossip and small talk it all up in their blogs.
Here the chickens, however, take it all in their stride
as if the world is one big joke, a cakewalk —
I've been especially impressed by the rooster;
sometimes I wonder if he has seen the future.
My father footers at something in the garden,
someone says something unimportant in the kitchen
to my mother's usual, love-full clatter of pans,
rattled to within an inch of their life,
the *Hollyoaks* theme tune comes from the living room
as loud as you like, as if there was no tomorrow —
you cannot hear the tick of a clock here —
ironically, you wouldn't catch me dead in there.
And tonight death seems like a million miles away
as I, perhaps, get closer to what it is I want to say.
And tonight the world feels like a million dollars,
and I feel the need for words like shebang,
arpeggio, carpaccio, Caravaggio,
piano, allegro, pimiento, bravado,
and in the garden everything seems so
abandoned, so easy-come easy-go:
the watering can has fallen on its side,
the daffodils are here, there and everywhere,
the spade against the ditch — a loner,
the deflated and faded *Gilbert* rugby ball,
unkicked, undrop-goaled, unconverted, untried,
tired, it lies beyond my brother's jinking,
dinking, running-rings-around-me, scoring,
reminds me of the games we used to play, one-on-one,
garryowening, chipping and chasing
our life away on an evening like this evening,
thirsts slaked by big pints of Robinsons *Orange Barley Water*,
a pause in play before we'd sidestep each other
until it couldn't get any darker

(older now, perhaps to grow is also to *out*grow;
older now, we find ourselves homesick at home),
as now my nephews' Disney slide is folded, horizontal
on the patch of grass it will keep from the rain and kill,
and beside the pampas grass beside the greenhouse
the midges seem left to their own devices:
a swarm of small sun-gods hovering en masse,
up to no good, a swathe of sunlit nuisance,
and the robin, alone, skitters through the leylandii
from one branch to another branch, inching,
shaking, then steadying, shaking, then steadying,
and I, for the life of me, can't tell you why
but remain gobsmacked at its balancing act,
its light-footed, easy-does-it, there-there, now-now knack,
the quiet science behind its body's equilibrium,
its give and take, tightrope-walker-like suspension,
which makes me see an order in the world, a system,
and think it's not so bad, it's not all doom and gloom.
And so, birds yap all through all the ash trees
as evening burns into the back of my head, recedes,
and so it is that I weigh things up, catch myself on —
second suns, one-off stars, robins, leylandii —
caught up in all the catchings of the eye.

## How to Live

Run in the morning. Read in the evening.
Eat little but well. Watch less TV.
Check email only once a day. Leave the house more.
Cook interesting meals. Make an effort
with old friends. Wear new clothes. Do something
you wouldn't. Fire a bet on a random horse.
Look, in greater depth, at the changes, so subtle,
in the faces of ageing friends, the scratches
on the surfaces of even the shiniest stuff.
Remember only the obligatory.
Chuck your green bottles in the green bottle bank.
Love only those who will love you back.

## London

*for Ahren Warner*

All great things flow towards the city,
said Aristotle, who, all told, you might agree,

had quite a lot to say for himself. But,
given the benefit of the doubt,

taking an open-minded standpoint,
it's easy to see what he was on about:

stand, at night, at Waterloo Bridge, for instance,
and bear witness to the Thames's dazzling genius

or note, there, the high-mindedness of the moon,
its certain smugness, its sort-of pretension.

But he didn't half blether on, Aristotle.
Look at these two chancers, out on the razzle,

now on a night-bus, out for the count, asleep,
as pissed as farts and missing their stop.

# Lagan from the Ormeau Bridge

You'll know when a sculler has been on the river:
the two-oared scuffed water catches, turns silver.

## Meandering

Alone today all along the river Aire
came back to me a girl I used to know:
the way she sipped at a cappuccino,

her ritual emptying of a sugar
with fingers made for the piano
as we sat in a brand new Belfast coffee bar.

But here I trudge the towpath's leftover snow
in the broken heart of a Yorkshire December,
think of time, water, love, where they go.

## Of All Things

The falling or the fallen leaf, of all things,
has been the emptiest that autumn brings,

summer's dilapidation laid bare on bare branches
(each second another of time's avalanches)

and the sunlight comes and the sunlight goes
and the world is a world of all things and shadows.

## New Year in Belfast

Ten in the morning on the Ormeau
at the start of another new year,
with bad breath and that just-out-of-bed look,
assessing the scuffs on my three-day-old Grensons
that are probably half a size too big,
checking the time through my scratched Skagen
I bought for myself as a birthday present
and thinking my lambswool scarf could do with a wash,
I waited for a bus opposite L'Etoile,
beside Ferguson Flowers and the Hungry Hound 2,
down a bit from the Orange Hall and the Chinese
and the offy and the two cashpoints
opposite where the Curzon used to be,
as men with pot bellies, high blood pressure
and smoker's coughs wend their way home
or to the bookie's, or cough or give me a look
as they pass, as a girl in her trackies
does anything but give me a look,
stubs her cig out on a bin and leaves it there
and moves on into the morning in her own time
as I go nowhere and wonder
if I'm at the right stop, if the buses are running,
if the bus will stop, if I've got change
which I do as I unearth, untangle
an Ulster Bank fiver from last night's bar receipts
and ask is this the start, the end, or just the same.

## River Run

There is something meaningful about a river
like this, on a Sunday morning like this,
at the start of a November like this
with the leaves falling and the sunlight strong
like this, with the water neither flowing
nor still, like this, and the dogs on leashes
like this, with cyclists zooming past
like that,
         runners losing their breath, like this.

# Acknowledgements

Thanks are due to the editors of the following publications in which these poems, or versions of them, appeared for the first time: *Brick, The Dark Horse, Horizon Review, The Manchester Review, The Moth, Poetry Ireland Review, Poetry London, Poetry Review, The Red Wheelbarrow, The Rialto, The Salt Book of Younger Poets, The SHOp, The Stinging Fly, The Sunday Tribune, The Ulster Tatler* and *The Yellow Nib*.

Several of the poems in this book were previously published in a pamphlet, *The Bus from Belfast* (Templar, 2011).

I am grateful to the UK Young Artists organization which selected me to represent the UK in Rome at the 2011 International Biennale of Young Artists. I gratefully acknowledge the support of the Northern Ireland Arts Council for awarding me a SIAP Award in 2009, the New York Residency in 2011 and the ACES Award in 2012.

I also wish to thank the following for helping shape this book in one way or another: my family, Niall Campbell, Ciaran Carson, Joe Loudon, Roddy Lumsden, David Park, Don Paterson, Damian Smyth, Jonathan Travis, Ahren Warner and Ben Wilkinson. Special thanks go to Peter Fallon.